Strategic Balancing Using Factual Data

Dinesh Jindal; Abhinav Aggarwal

authorHOUSE®

AuthorHouse™
1663 Liberty Drive
Bloomington, IN 47403
www.authorhouse.com
Phone: 1 (800) 839-8640

Front Cover Image © Rawpixelimages | Dreamstime.com
Back cover image © Ratz Attila | Dreamstime.com

Published by AuthorHouse 02/14/2018

ISBN: 978-1-5462-1691-9 (sc)
ISBN: 978-1-5462-1690-2 (e)

Library of Congress Control Number: 2017918612

Print information available on the last page.

This book is printed on acid-free paper.

for my family:

Sumi Jindal, wife
Dr. Kittu Jindal Garg and Isha Jindal Sharma, daughters
Dr. Akash Garg and Dr. Avishkar Sharma, sons-in-law
Aanya Garg, grand daughter

Dinesh Jindal

for my mentor, research guide, and friend Prof. Subhash Wadhwa

Abhinav Aggarwal

Foreword

Jim McKeighan
Executive Strategic Advisor
linkedin.com/in/jimmckeighan

"Strategy is a high level <u>plan</u> to achieve one or more goals under conditions of uncertainty. Strategy is important because the resources available to achieve these goals are usually limited."[1]

All of us, including the C-suite, are challenged with defining a logical approach that quickly gets our team on the same page towards developing our Strategies. This is not easy, and the complexity has continued to compound by the pace of change from our Global Economy, to new Business Models and the increasing rapid change of Information Technologies capabilities.

I have had the opportunity to work with several F500 organizations as a Strategic Advisor while I was at Bearingpoint, Computer Sciences Corporation, KPMG, Oracle Corporation and Unisys Corporation. As a senior executive with extensive experience in business incubation, industry and technology consulting, large-scale transformations, outsourcing and most recently enterprise cloud strategies – I have worked on numerous strategies of varying scope. Throughout my career I have been exposed to many books, approaches, frameworks, tools, templates and the like for Strategic Planning. In the end, I have found that all the best strategies I worked on were a result of:

- engaged *Executive Sponsors* and Governance,
- committing the *best Team* across all required disciplines (not just who is available).

- gathering as input the _best possible Data_ across all the factors to be considered, and
- using a _logical and simple Approach_ that helped the team weigh and balance this data, in a manner that resulted in the formation of an executable Strategy

In addition, a frequent issue I have seen many times is the misalignment between the Business and Information Technology domains of a strategy. They cannot be addressed serially or as an afterthought of the other. They must be done together, in an integrated fashion. This will not only result in a better Strategy, but it will actually expedite arriving at the Strategy and subsequent execution of it.

Dinesh and Abhinav have developed a very practical approach to Strategic Planning that deals with many challenges, issues and gaps that commonly exist. I have known Dinesh for many years since our client consulting engagements at Unisys Corporation. Dinesh has always had a unique ability to take the complex and frame it in a comprehensive, yet simple manner. His experiences on multiple client engagements across industry sectors and various geographies have placed him in a unique position to do the same for Strategic Balancing.

This book is both a must read and great reference tool for anyone developing a multi-faceted Strategy that requires the balancing of multiple stakeholders, business, operations, technology and constraining factors.

[1] Wikipedia.

Strategic Balancing Using Factual Data

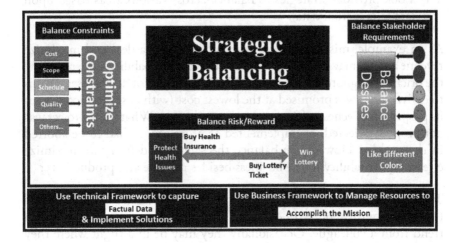

Preface

Every business has various segments (business units or teams) and the mission of each segment leader is to provide best value for their individual segment. Does that provide an overall effective profitability to the business based upon their mission, vision and various tangible/intangible factors? This book provides strategies to balance across various areas based upon real data (aka factual data).

As an example, mission of sales segment is to win a deal and maximize revenue and we may promise a project without our capability, underestimate the pricing, or ignore an important risk. The mission of delivery segment is to deliver what was promised at the lowest cost (with best productivity for its proper effectiveness, efficiency, and consistency). What if the project was not properly selected, or implemented as promised, or had to be aborted in the middle? How do we balance the sales and delivery to maximize effective profitability to the business besides revenue and productivity?

Typically, business leaders are quite busy. They have no time to read tutorials, lengthy reports, or even to get an overview on a current technical trend from a colleague. Occasionally they may be in a flight where they can open a kindle, nook, or an iPad to read a book or an article of interest. This book is written with a busy executive in mind, one who is juggling between priorities, and fighting several fires simultaneously. Since various leaders may have completely different backgrounds, this book requires no pre-requisites.

The term business may mean a business entity, corporation, company, government, family, social group, or even a religious entity and this book is intended for all their leaders. This book might refer to them as business or company.

This book provides various strategic balancing factors. Since a leader is not expected to have proper background knowledge of all technical/business areas under balancing factors, this book provides basic knowledge about technical and business areas with no expected background, including pictorial formats with daily life analogies where applicable; followed by basic high-level knowledge for major state-of-the-art technical and business areas.

Although it covers majority of technical and business frameworks, it doesn't provide full technical details for any topic needed for actual technical processing. It provides just basic information needed for business leaders to get an understanding of the big picture and help them in taking appropriate decisions with real-life analogies based upon factual data. If they need any further details for any technical topic, they can request their appropriate team members. Moreover, none of the sub-sections requires any pre-requisites.

Another way to look at a business purpose is **What, Why and How**. In other words:

- **What** should be promised/delivered?
- **Why** to promise/deliver this i.e. does it accomplish the short-term/ long-term goals for our business/customers?
- **How** do we plan to accomplish this, and ensure that besides performance of each segment, are they properly balanced based upon their integration, factual data, real-time status; and what action needs to be taken to deliver and continue improvement over time?

One of the best ways to decide what, why, and how - is by means of Business Case analysis and compare Cost/Benefit for all options based upon various tangible and intangible factors. Some of the parameters may change over time but if the decision has to made now, one has to decide based upon current known parameters.

This book is divided into 3 sections and each section includes various subsections and chapters.

- Section 1 analyzes overall profitability for business via strategic balancing based upon factual data
- Section 2 provides the framework and high-level understanding of various technical areas for the leaders including: Infrastructure, Data/Big Data, Enterprise Architecture, with a base for Enterprise Mobility, and Enterprise Security. Technical framework is needed to capture factual data as well to implement the strategy
- Section 3 provides the framework and high-level understanding of various business areas for the leaders including: Strategy/ Tactics/Operations, Sales/Pre-Sales, Project Management, Service Management, and Quality Management. Business framework is needed to manage all activities as per requirements.

This book forms the basis and subject material for a course that is available in web format with presentations and recorded sessions for each section.

Authors can be contacted to deliver an interactive workshop with hands-on exercises to resolve real-world business problems using an approach outlined in this book.

Table of Contents

SECTION 1: Strategic Balancing 1

Sub-Section 1.1– Provide proper framework for Balancing 2
Chapter 1.1.1 (Collaboration) 2
Chapter 1.1.2 (Visibility) 3
Chapter 1.1.3 (Dynamic Redistribution) 3
Chapter 1.1.4 (Business Case Analysis) 3

Sub-Section 1.2– Balancing across Business Area Segments 5
Chapter 1.2.1 (Balance Sales vs. Delivery) 6
Chapter 1.2.2 (Balance Market Side vs. Supply Side) 9
Chapter 1.2.3 (Balance Existing Clients vs. Attracting New Customers) 9
Chapter 1.2.4 (Balance Productivity vs. Profitability) 10
Chapter 1.2.5 (Balance Short-term vs. Long-term goals) 15
Chapter 1.2.6 (Balance External vs. Internal Requirements) 16
Chapter 1.2.7 (Balance Productivity vs. Operational Overhead) 17
Chapter 1.2.8 (Balance Bureaucracy vs. Flexibility) 18
Chapter 1.2.9 (Balance Outsourcing vs. Insourcing) 19
Chapter 1.2.10 (Balance Project Management vs. People Management) 22
Chapter 1.2.11 (Balance Inter vs. Intra Project Collaboration) 22
Chapter 1.2.12 (Balance Quality vs. Quantity) 24
Chapter 1.2.13 (Balance Content vs. Formatting) 25
Chapter 1.2.14 (Balance Perception vs. Reality) 26
Chapter 1.2.15 (Balance As-Is vs. To-Be scenario) 26
Chapter 1.2.16 (Balance Actions vs. Outcome) 28
Chapter 1.2.17 (Balance Passion vs. Practicality) 29
Chapter 1.2.18 (Balance Innovation vs. Reality) 29
Chapter 1.2.19 (Balance Crazy vs. Non-crazy workers) 30
Chapter 1.2.20 (Balance Local vs. Remote employee assignments) 31
Chapter 1.2.21 (Balance under pressure vs. not under pressure) 31
Chapter 1.2.22 (Balance Similar vs. different team opinions/ approach) 31
Chapter 1.2.23 (Balance working independently vs. with team) 31
Chapter 1.2.24 (Balance across multiple Domains) 32
Chapter 1.2.25 (Leader vs. Manager) 33

Sub-Section 1.3– Improve over time 34
Chapter 1.3.1 (Ensure quantitative improvements over time) 34

Chapter 1.3.2 (Continual Tool Improvements)............................ 34

Chapter 1.3.3 (Continual Process Improvements) 35

Sub-Section 1.4– Summary of Strategic Balancing......................**37**

SECTION 2: Technical Framework **43**

Sub Section 2.1– Technical Base **45**

Chapter 2.1.1. Hardware.. 45

Chapter 2.1.2. Infrastructure 47

Chapter 2.1.3. Network 49

Chapter 2.1.4. Software 50

Chapter 2.1.5. Cloud Computing... 52

Sub Section 2.2– Data and Big Data...**60**

Chapter 2.2.1. Data Management... 60

Chapter 2.2.2. Hierarchical Model: 61

Chapter 2.2.3. Network Model:.. 62

Chapter 2.2.4. Relational Model... 62

Chapter 2.2.5. Data Normalization and Modeling...................... 67

Chapter 2.2.6. Transactional Database 72

Chapter 2.2.7. Data Warehouse 74

Chapter 2.2.8. ETL (Extraction, Transformation, and Loading)
Process 84

Chapter 2.2.9. Data Migration Quality.. 92

Chapter 2.2.10. Data Sync-up (Data Bridging) 96

Chapter 2.2.11. Business Intelligence 97

Chapter 2.2.12. Data Mining 98

Chapter 2.2.13. Big Data 101

Chapter 2.2.14. Data Lakes... 107

Chapter 2.2.15. Business Analytics... 108

Chapter 2.2.16. Big Data and Cloud...110

Chapter 2.2.17. Common Tools/Technologies related to Data: 112

Chapter 2.2.18. Tools/Technologies for Big Data:.......................113

Sub-Section 2.3– Enterprise Architecture **116**

Chapter 2.3.1. Service-Oriented Architecture (SOA):..................117

Chapter 2.3.2. Reference, Target, and Existing Architecture:.......118

Chapter 2.3.3. Emerging trends and future-vision architecture: ...119

Sub-Section 2.4– Enterprise Mobility.......................................**125**

Sub-Section 2.5– Enterprise Security..**127**

Sub-Section 2.6– Summary of Technical Framework **129**

SECTION 3: Business Framework 132

Sub-Section 3.1– Accomplish Mission with Strategy, Tactics, Operations 133

Sub-Section 3.2– Sales/Pre-Sales 135
Chapter 3.2.1. Balance Sales/Delivery: 135
Chapter 3.2.2. Co-relate Sales/Delivery/Operations and their Historic Data 136
Chapter 3.2.3. Impress Business/Technical Leaders of Potential Customers: 137
Chapter 3.2.4. Minimize Sales/Pre-Sales expenses: 139
Chapter 3.2.5. Proof of Concept (Prototyping) 140
Chapter 3.2.6. Go-to-market (GTM) i.e. What to Sell 140
Chapter 3.2.7. Market Dynamics i.e. how much to price? 140
Chapter 3.2.8. POV (Point of View) i.e. How Real is what we recommend? 141
Chapter 3.2.9. Negotiation: 141

Sub-Section 3.3– Project Management 142
Chapter 3.3.1. Purpose of Project Management 142
Chapter 3.3.2. Water Fall vs. Iterative/Agile Methodologies 144
Chapter 3.3.3. Water Fall Project Management 145
Chapter 3.3.4. Iterative/Agile Project Management 162
Chapter 3.3.5. Scrum 163
Chapter 3.3.6. Rational Unified Process (RUP) 164
Chapter 3.3.7. The Unified Modeling Language (UML) 168

Sub-Section 3.4– IT Service Management 176
Chapter 3.4.1. Purpose of ITIL: 177
Chapter 3.4.2. Important ITIL Terms: 178
Chapter 3.4.3. Service Strategy: 180
Chapter 3.4.4. Service Design: 183
Chapter 3.4.5. Service Transition: 187
Chapter 3.4.6. Service Operation: 190
Chapter 3.4.7. Continual Service Improvement: 192
Chapter 3.4.8. Functions 193

Sub-Section 3.5– Quality/Waste Management 196

Sub-Section 3.6– Summary of Business Framework 199

All Diagrams

Fig 1.0 Strategic Balancing..1
Fig 1.1 Optimize Profitability..2
Fig 1.2 Balancing across Business Area Segments 5
Fig 1.2.1 Main Purpose of Project Management 10
Fig 1.2.2 Overuse of Resources.. 13
Fig 1.2.3 Productivity and Operational Overhead.................17
Fig 1.2.4 Process Lifecycle 18
Fig 1.2.5 Overall Project Collaboration............................. 24
Fig 1.2.6 Solutioning Components 28
Fig 1.2.7 Leaders versus Managers.................................... 33

Fig 2.0 Technical Framework 43
Fig 2.1 Technical Base..45
Fig 2.1.1 A PC mother board (image courtesy: Pixabay) 46
Fig 2.1.2 A memory card 46
Fig 2.1.3 NAND gate and truth table............................... 47
Fig 2.1.4 A conceptual view of hardware, software, and
network 48
Fig 2.1.5 HA fail over of resource group 49
Fig 2.1.6 User/Device Connection.................................... 50
Fig 2.1.7 Software Stack 51
Fig 2.1.8 (Table): public, private, and hybrid cloud
characteristics 56
Fig 2.1.9 The Organic Cloud Evolution Ecosystem............... 58
Fig 2.1.10 A simple cloud computing Governance Model 59
Fig 2.2 Data and Big Data..60
Fig 2.2.1 Hierarchical Model.. 62
Fig 2.2.2 Network Model 62
Fig 2.2.3 Relational Model 63
Fig 2.2.4 RDBMS Sample 65
Fig 2.2.5 Unnormalized Data 67
Fig 2.2.6 First Normal Form-Primary Key 68
Fig 2.2.7 Second Normal Form 69
Fig 2.2.8 Third Normal Form 69
Fig 2.2.9 E-R Diagram 70
Fig 2.2.10 Conceptual Data Model.................................... 70
Fig 2.2.11 Logical Data Model 71
Fig 2.2.12 Physical Data Model.. 72
Fig 2.2.13 Dimension and Fact Tables 77
Fig 2.2.14 Star Schema 78

Fig 2.2.15 Snowflake Schema 78
Fig 2.2.16 Fact Constellation Schema 79
Fig 2.2.17 Legacy Data Migration 85
Fig 2.2.18 Transactional Data to Data Warehouse Migration . 85
Fig 2.2.19 Source Data Summary 88
Fig 2.2.20 Source Data Relationships 88
Fig 2.2.21 Source Data Details 89
Fig 2.2.22 Data Transformation 89
Fig 2.2.23 Logical Data Map 91
Fig 2.2.24 Application Modernization 97
Fig 2.2.25 Big Data Example 104
Fig 2.2.26 Data Lakes 108
Fig 2.2.27 When to Buy 109
Fig 2.2.28 When to Sell 110
Fig 2.2.29 Future Big Data and Cloud Potential Idea 111
Fig 2.3 Enterprise Architecture 116
Fig 2.3.1 Service-Oriented Architecture (SOA) 118
Fig 2.3.2 When to develop a Microservice 120
Fig 2.3.3 Towards evolution of the ecosystem with examples of
reusability 123
Fig 2.3.4 Example of a simplified future-vision architecture . 124
Fig 2.4 Enterprise Mobility 125

Fig 3.0 Business Framework 132
Fig 3.1 Accomplish Mission with Strategy, ... 133
Fig 3.2 Sales/Pre-Sales 135
Fig 3.2.1 Co-relate WBS Codes across Lifecycle 137
Fig 3.2.2 Pictorial Walk Through 138
Fig 3.2.3 Pictorial Walk-Through Impresses Business Leaders 139
Fig 3.3 Project Management 143
Fig 3.3.1 Waterfall versus Iterative/Agile Methodology 145
Fig 3.3.2 Rolling Wave Planning 146
Fig 3.3.3 Waterfall Methodology 148
Fig 3.3.4 Activity Dependency 151
Fig 3.3.5 Critical Path 152
Fig 3.3.6 Functional Organization Structure 154
Fig 3.3.7 Projectized Organization Structure 155
Fig 3.3.8 Matrix Organization Structure 155
Fig 3.3.9 OCBC Center Singapore 163
Fig 3.3.10 Scrum Methodology 163
Fig 3.3.11 Rational Unified Process (RUP) 165
Fig 3.3.12 Use Case Diagram 169
Fig 3.3.13 Activity Diagram 169

Fig 3.3.14 State Machine Diagram...170
Fig 3.3.15 Communication/Collaboration Diagram...............170
Fig 3.3.16 Sequence Diagram 171
Fig 3.3.17 Class Diagram..171
Fig 3.3.18 Object Diagram 172
Fig 3.3.19 Component Diagram 172
Fig 3.3.20 Deployment Diagram 173
Fig 3.3.21 Package Diagram 173
Fig 3.3.22 Timing Diagram...174
Fig 3.3.23 Interaction Overview Diagram 174
Fig 3.3.24 Composite Structure Diagram 175
Fig 3.4 Service Management.. 176
Fig 3.4.1 Service Portfolio..182
Fig 3.4.2 Service Design 183
Fig 3.4.3 Service Catalog 185
Fig 3.4.4 Availability Management Times............................. 186
Fig 3.4.5 Information Security Management 186
Fig 3.4.6 Service Knowledge Management System (SKMS)...189
Fig 3.4.7 Continual Service Improvement.............................193

SECTION 1

Strategic Balancing

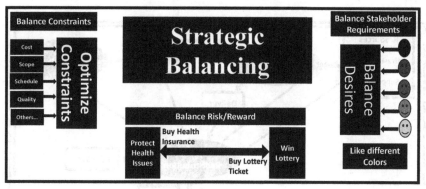

Fig 1.0 Strategic Balancing

Sub-Section 1.1

Provide proper framework for Balancing

Regardless of whether you are leading people, infrastructure, data, services, projects…, you need a framework for four areas i.e.

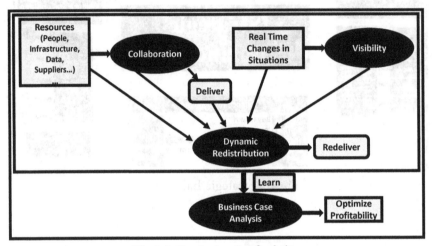

Fig 1.1 Optimize Profitability

Chapter 1.1.1 (Collaboration)

Provide best utilization by collaboration across various resources within your domain i.e.

- As a people manager, collaborate across all individuals
- As the infrastructure lead, collaborate across all hardware resources and their providers
- As a data lead, collaborate across all data sources
- As a service lead, collaborate across all services…
- As a project manager, collaborate across all above areas

Do we have the proper framework that can integrate across all people, tools, technology, data, communications, locations, and others in real-time so that we can visualize what's happening and act accordingly?

One has to build proper plans to collaborate across various areas.

Chapter 1.1.2 (Visibility)

Besides proper framework to collaborate, we need to find the real-time visibility of all resources. In other words, if a person becomes unavailable, a server falls down, data gets corrupted, service becomes unavailable, strike takes place with a supplier, or even the project manager becomes unavailable – it must be visible in real-time to take proper action. If there are many events going on, what needs to be visible first may also be prioritized based upon various factors.

Find out how to utilize technology and processes to collect proper data so that decisions can be data-driven based upon factual data. Sub Section 2.2 provides details about data, big data, and data analytics.

If any action takes place, there must be proper means to capture relevant data and join with other data, analyze them and send proper information as real-time visibility to proper individuals.

Chapter 1.1.3 (Dynamic Redistribution)

Once we have the real-time visibility, we must re-collaborate and re-distribute resources in real time i.e. dynamic re-distribution to achieve best result.

Optimize how to use the mission with collaboration and visibility of actual situation and dynamically redistribute various resources in real-time to maximize productivity.

Use proper mindset or tools (spreadsheet or more complex analytic tools) to find the best way to re-distribute various resources dynamically based upon real-time situation and act accordingly. One way to find the best result is via Cost/Benefit analysis shown next.

Chapter 1.1.4 (Business Case Analysis)

Perform a cost/benefit analysis to ensure our dynamic re-distribution provides best results. Moreover, learn from past experience and improve the process for collaboration, visibility, dynamic redistribution as needed based upon various practical factors within your business.

Compares Cost/Benefit for various options based upon tangible and intangible factors.

Although for immediate action, one can find a work-around to redistribute various resources, for proper problem resolution, one has to provide proper balancing across various areas based upon current and past data plus predictive and prescriptive analytics for future actions.

Best example could be supply-chain situation. One needs to find out all suppliers and consumers of any product across the world and plan properly. In reality, if there's an earthquake or a strike at one of the supplier/consumer locations, one has to get that information quickly and take immediate steps to find best alternative.

Another example: Let's consider a huge store chain. First of all, there needs to be full co-ordination planned across all stores, locations, employees, suppliers, manufacturers, leaders and others (**Collaboration**). If in some chain stores at a particular location, suddenly there's unexpected big sale of a product, that information has to be captured within a reasonable time to a data repository and be available to the proper individuals (**Visibility**). Proper steps need to be taken to ensure enough supply of the product in that location (**Dynamic Redistribution**). Finally, perhaps most importantly, there needs to be proper analysis as to why there was unexpected big sale and use that input for future planning (**Business Case Analysis**).

Sub-Section 1.2

Balancing across Business Area Segments

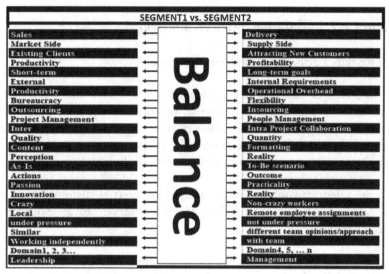

SEGMENT1 vs. SEGMENT2		
Sales	Balance	Delivery
Market Side		Supply Side
Existing Clients		Attracting New Customers
Productivity		Profitability
Short-term		Long-term goals
External		Internal Requirements
Productivity		Operational Overhead
Bureaucracy		Flexibility
Outsourcing		Insourcing
Project Management		People Management
Inter		Intra Project Collaboration
Quality		Quantity
Content		Formatting
Perception		Reality
As-Is		To-Be scenario
Actions		Outcome
Passion		Practicality
Innovation		Reality
Crazy		Non-crazy workers
Local		Remote employee assignments
under pressure		not under pressure
Similar		different team opinions/approach
Working independently		with team
Domain 1, 2, 3...		Domain 4, 5, ... n
Leadership		Management

Fig 1.2 Balancing across Business Area Segments

It's extremely important to decide actions based upon factual data as one of the major input.

No activity is complete unless we can measure it

- Maintain performance metrics over time to check directional movements
- Define standard best practices and maintain their compliance rating for each activity
- Ensure the correctness of the captured data? One way could be to use two conflicting parties and let one of the parties capture the data and then the other party can verify it
- Once captured, use these to build KPIs (Key Performance Indicator), to balance scorecard for future use, and KRI (Key Risk Indicator) to control risk
- Keep analyzing based upon past history and improve processes accordingly

This sub-section covers the main purpose of the book i.e. how to maximize the strategic balancing across various factors and maintain proper cost/benefit analysis to ensure that all actions are practical based upon various tangible and intangible factors.

Chapter 1.2.1 (Balance Sales vs. Delivery)

Once we win a deal, we enhance our revenue.

Once we deliver the product/service with proper collaboration across various areas at minimum overall cost, we maximize productivity. If we choose the wrong product, regardless of the success of delivery, it doesn't achieve the profitability. If we choose the proper product but not able to deliver it properly or had to abort in the middle, still no proper profitability.

The term client can refer to both external or internal customers and the word sales can also refer to selling a product/service to an external or internal customer.

What happens if we promise to sell a product/service that we are not capable of delivering, or we promise to sell at a cost that is lower than the actual cost – resulting in loss, or our estimates are too high that we fail to win the deal and we waste money on sale, or we underestimate/overestimate a major risk.

All these factors end up in either wasting money on sales, losing money on delivery, or aborting delivery in the middle and losing even more money. Moreover, even if we deliver the product/service perfectly but the product/service was not properly selected based upon various short/long-term factors – it's a waste of money. Like if instead of performing a medical surgery on the left leg, by mistake we instruct the doctor to perform the surgery on the right leg. Even if the operation is perfect – what's the outcome?

What really matters is the TCO (Total Cost of Ownership) that includes the cost for entire lifecycle of an entity and its return/profitability. There are various ways to compute the Net Present Value based upon when and what value we spend/achieve. TCO may include all expenses including capital expense to build the framework, operational overheads, marketing cost, cost for product/project; and Operational cost. It may also include various indirect costs including money spent on sales that we couldn't win, common money spent on real-estate etc. Similarly, for returns some products/projects can be used as a common base/intellectual property for other entities and one should include short-term/long-term returns. A typical example of TCO from a user's perspective is a car and its effective annual cost is computed based upon all money spent on initial cost, fuel, insurance, maintenance, repairs, service, loans, interest on loan payments as well as final worth of the car after a fixed period. Of course, we need to include various intangible factors like comfort level of the car, its security, its branding, color etc.

This chapter covers four main areas that maximize the probability of 'what we promise - gets delivered at expected profitability'.

1. Promise based upon our capability:

If we are not capable of delivering what we promised, it may have various negative effects including:

- We might have to abort delivery in the middle wasting all money spent
- We might have to pay penalty to the client due to some compromise or legal action
- It can create lot of business expenses/frustration to team members with lay-offs
- We may lose 'time to market' for other important products
- It may impact our confidence level to our clients and thus we may lose future sales

Once we understand the client requirements, we need to check with appropriate teams to ensure that it can be architected, designed, implemented, tested, deployed, supported, and documented. Moreover, just checking with other teams may not be enough. It's also important to capture all historic data and use that data as a base to check of any issues where we were not able to deliver similar tasks and what actions we have taken/should take to resolve those issues. As an example, before we promise 99.9% reliability of a service, we should use our current technology and factual data both as main inputs.

2. Provide proper cost estimates based upon past delivery

If to provide the cost estimate for a task, we check with our subject matter experts and they think it will take 100 hours to complete the task and we price it accordingly. But, if we have done same (or similar) task many times in the past and it has never taken less than

1,000 hours, shouldn't we use our past experience as a realistic input in addition to collaborating with our subject matter experts? Same may be true the other way around i.e. we estimate it 1,000 hours and lose the deal although historically it has never taken more than 100 hours to complete similar task. If we underquote, we may lose money on delivery and if we overquote we may waste money on sales and not win the deal.

3. Provide proper risks based upon past history and their associated cost estimates

Let's say we have a risk defined as high probability and we increase the price quote accordingly (i.e. using Estimated Monetary Value i.e. EMV). But we have used same risk many times in the past over multiple tasks and it has rarely become an issue, shouldn't we reduce the risk probability based upon factual data and not overquote unnecessarily?

Similarly, the risk can be shown as low probability, but it has often become an issue many times and again becomes a major issue and we lose substantial money on its delivery, or may have to abort the project since the risk was not anticipated.

4. Use proper tools to capture data

Let's say we are using local copy of spreadsheet as data to provide cost estimate or risks for a deal. That may have many issues including:

- Difficult to maintain fact-based metrics over time
- Difficult to consolidate data across different areas, compute total cost, remove duplicates
- Difficult to build analytic reporting for different lines of business
- Difficult to reuse data for different sales
- Avoid multiple tool versions being used by different individuals and maintain their consistency
- Maintain data confidentiality/security i.e. anyone can share cost estimate (spreadsheet) even with our competitors
- Maintenance/accuracy of the tool without impacting its end users
- Allow concurrent updates by multiple users

We should use centralized data/logic and web-based interface for data capture, analysis, and reporting – although we can still use local spreadsheet (or other tools) for local use.

Refer to sub-section 3.2 (Sales/Pre-Sales) that provides best way to achieve sales/pre-sales profitability; and Chapter 1.2.4 (Balance Productivity vs. Profitability) to achieve maximum profitability for delivery.

Chapter 1.2.2 (Balance Market Side vs. Supply Side)

What happens if a US Car manufacturer (right-hand drive) decides to sell left-hand steering wheel cars to Japan (left-hand drive)?

- Market-side provides what's needed by the market or customers
- Supply-side provides what we can supply

It's no use of trying to market a product that we can supply but the market doesn't need. Similarly, if market needs a product and we supply completely different type of product, it may not be worth selling that product.

Best case would be to produce what the market needs and only if we are capable to supply that product. Moreover, we should ensure that we and our customers both achieve overall TCO profitability.

Refer to sub-section 3.2 (Sales/Pre-Sales) for important Market-Side factors.

Chapter 1.2.3 (Balance Existing Clients vs. Attracting New Customers)

There's a substantial cost involved in attracting new customers and perhaps even a bigger cost if we lose existing customers (Churn).

The churn rate, is the percentage of subscribers to a service who discontinue their subscriptions within a given time period. For a company to expand its growth and clients, the number of new customers must exceed its churn rate for proper balancing.

To attract new customers, it's pretty common that companies offer special offer to new customers (only new customers and not existing customers). Let's say a telecom company X offers free (or almost free) deal for a long period to attract new customers for a telecom (internet/ phone) service. If that provides great attraction for company Y customers to join company X – X company may add new customers and Y company may lose existing customers. In other words, as companies' X and Y offer those deals, total number of customers don't change for either company but both companies lose a substantial amount as part of special offers and the overheads.

It's important to balance the special offers in a way not just to attract new customers but also to retain existing customers - although it's difficult since once we attract new customers, that means our competitors are also going to attract our existing customers. So, this should be balanced based upon our product/service specialty and should have two separate policies to attract our competitor's customers along with an additional policy to retain our existing customers.

Chapter 1.2.4 (Balance Productivity vs. Profitability)

Project Management is mainly aimed at operational cost containment

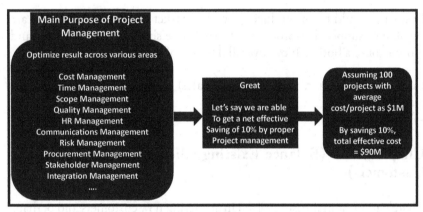

Fig 1.2.1 Main Purpose of Project Management

- According to PMI study: only ~34% of the projects get through completion
- In other words, all the effort on 66% of the projects is a pure waste
- (besides legal issues, frustration, layoffs if the project aborts in the middle...)
- If we stop initiating those 66% projects
- Net Cost $34M (less 10% additional savings via PM cost containment) = $30.6M

Huge savings from $90M to $34M (without 10% savings) to $30.6M (with 10% savings)

- Even if we can stop initiating just half of the 66% projects
Net Cost $100M - $33M = $67M (less 10% via cost containment)
= $60.3M

Still huge savings from $90M to $67M to $60.3M

Cost Containment is primarily aimed at **internal efficiency** and productivity

Whereas **Value Generation** is aimed at **external efficiency** to maximize profitability (value)

How to control project initiation to maximize value generation and effective profitability by minimizing the probability of aborting the project before completion?

Here are 7 main suggestions:

1. Appropriate Buy-In from leadership teams

Example: Let's say our business is using local spreadsheets for majority of very important global data that may have various issues. We create tools that are based upon centralized data and web-based user interface where we can easily maintain all factual metrics over time, that can provide real great value for the business.

But due to whatever reason, if the authority of the business wants to continue using local spreadsheets - what will happen next? Most likely the project will abort or not implemented and all the effort to convert local spreadsheets to new tool is wasted.

Therefore, despite other logical factors and even if one can prove that this has the best cost/benefit profitability, unless you have the buy-in from the leadership team, it may have no impact. So, it's very important to convince the appropriate leaders and move ahead only if they approve the next step. If the leadership team doesn't want to change, it's more practical to collaborate with them, rather than making futile effort to swim against the current.

2. Understanding of the Client Needs

- What happens if we sell a great product at a great price but didn't realize, that it may be against a particular religion and we try to sell the product to that religious group?
- What happened if we sell very large size clothes (greater than 6 feet height) to a region where majority of people are under 6 feet?
- Similarly, from operational stand point, we provide the best help desk support in English but the customers don't understand English?

In short, it's extremely important not to waste any effort in achieving result without satisfying the client.

3. Proper Framework to control Scope Creep

Scope Creep refers to change of scope for a project compared to what was intended initially when the project started. We can't assume that the requirements won't change after we start a project. While it's practical to allow changes, changes may have various impact including costing, regulation, compatibility, timing, resources etc.

It's important to provide a suitable framework to capture proper input and analyze them and act accordingly for any scope creep. Here are some details needed for the framework:

- The new change must be authorized by the project sponsor (in-charge)
- Find its impact to related or even unrelated tasks/projects or regulations
- Find the related risks/rewards
- Find who will contribute for any additional cost/benefit
- Estimate the effective additional cost and return and complete cost/benefit analysis
- Record required data
- Provide proper communication to related parties

4. Resource Availability

If there are 5 lanes on a road, but the number of parallel vehicles trying to move is much more than 5, overall movement success is much worse than even if we had just two lanes and each lane has only one vehicle moving

Fig 1.2.2 Overuse of Resources

in parallel. Of course, higher the lanes, better the result, but if there are no proper rules to control the traffic, that makes it even worse. Even a highway can quickly turn to look like a parking lot if traffic flow is more than what it can handle (like the above diagram) and it is not controlled.

Same is true for resource management. One should initiate parallel projects based upon resource availability.

It is not uncommon to observe this on large and complex projects where requirements gathering by itself has become a never-ending exercise (kind of Analysis-Paralysis). Isolated odd cases have consumed the entire project budget and still gathering requirements after 10 years as they have no governance in place and keep changing requirements all the time.

One of the ways to address this problem is to capture requirements within the tool (like a business process model) and play it back to key stake-holders to buy in and agree, and modify on the fly during playback to accommodate suggested changes. Prioritizing and dividing the project in small byte sized chunks, each one as a user story that can be accommodated in an agile methodology project backlog and iterated towards perfection would be one of the preferred ways to deal with such complexity and size. Refer to Chapter 3.3.2 (Water Fall vs. Iterative/Agile Methodologies).

Regardless, it's more practical to have appropriate projects in parallel based upon availability of various resources.

5. Proper communication management framework

Since multiple tasks are dependent upon each other, it is very important for task B to know if something changes for task A. If there is a sudden disaster in a location where a supplier is located, it's important for others to know to make a dynamic redistribution decision.

Therefore, it's important to provide a framework that allows proper communication as needed.

6. Ensure proper Project-Mix

If we have same number of data engineering and infrastructure technical experts, but most of our projects are needing infrastructure resources, we are wasting our resources; or we have only one type of resources whereas our projects need all type of resources.

Similarly, if all our projects are based upon one type of market although we provide multiple markets and something happens to that specific market, we are wasting all our resources.

We should provide project mix – i.e. multiple projects based upon resources needs/availability; market diversity based upon our specialty, short-term/long-term goals, and many other parameters that help us to diversify and optimize dependency.

7. Delivery based upon client's satisfaction

Let's say we want to deliver 100 units of a new product in 10 months to a new customer. One way could be to deliver 10 units per month which may be suitable for operational requirements.

When we are working on a new project, it may be more important to build a prototype or sample first and keep improving it till client gets satisfied, then enhance the delivery as we go and increase number of units/month. Let's say, we may even take 6 months to deliver the first product that's liked by the customer and then deliver higher number over the remaining period (that may keep going up as we achieve better client satisfaction).

All these factors are important to minimize the probability of project abortion before completion and thus balancing of cost containment (productivity) with value generation (profitability)

From data capture point of view, it's important to keep proper relationship for all activities related to entire life cycle of any product/service including sales, delivery, and ongoing operational expenses and revenue including any project that has to be aborted in the middle. That will provide best TCO (Total Cost of Ownership) and help both the customer and supplier.

Chapter 1.2.5 (Balance Short-term vs. Long-term goals)

Typically, we aim at resource utilization of products/services per hour/(some short period). That certainly provides us short-term benefit but if the resources are not compatible with long-term requirements – does that provide long-term benefit?

To ensure long-term benefit, we should also look at

- Quality of work
- Is the outcome in line with future expectations?
- Reuse of the products/services output and knowledge gained towards future needs

Main purpose of short-term goal is to ensure that:

- All staff hours are properly utilized
- All governance issues are resolved and frauds are detected
- Minimize customer churns where churn refers to existing clients leaving your company (products or services)
- All products/services are properly maintained

Main purpose of long-term goal should include:

- Build tools that can be reused multiple times based upon total cost to maximize ROI (Return on Investment)
- Retain staff for long-term retention and deployment on new projects to reduce immediate need for hiring new staff (especially if each new employee needs some training)
- Reuse resources (people, infrastructure, software, real-estate, intellectual property etc.) for long-term use

In short, we should ensure that short-term operational functions are compatible with long-term Sales, Engineering, and Financial requirements

Chapter 1.2.6 (Balance External vs. Internal Requirements)

External requirements are directly based upon any sales/delivery/services requirements – whether it's meant for an external/internal client, or for a product/service we are building for use as a generic product/service.

Internal requirements refer to maintaining all internal data with proper tools and resources to build historic patterns and analyze that data to continue making improvements relevant to external requirements.

Whereas external requirements are directly related to revenue, internal requirements are not directly related to revenue, but for the long term it can provide profitability over TCO.

How much time and money to spend on each internal requirement need to be properly balanced?

Maintaining strategic balancing for all areas covered in this sub-section is an example of internal requirements.

Here are some examples where capturing internal data within a business and analyzing it based upon internal requirements can enhance business profitability:

- Let's say we are leading a data/big data specialized consulting company and provide great value to our clients on how to capture, analyze, and utilize data to achieve best value. Do we use the same skills for our own internal business to ensure our sales/delivery are balanced, our timesheets are properly captured and all other data related to various areas are balanced? This is an example of providing data analytics for external requirements vs. capturing/analyzing data for internal requirements
- For any product, the total cost for a supplier should include all costs related to marketing/sales, delivery, and ongoing operations (TCO-Total Cost of Ownership).
  Do we maintain proper relationships between sales/delivery/operations to ease cost relationships? One easy and simple way could be to keep the coding (WBS Code) for time sheets in such a way that the WBS Code for the entire lifecycle of the product is related so that when the time sheets are captured, the relationship allows automatic capture of TCO. Refer to Chapter 3.2.2. (Co-relate Sales/Delivery/Operations and their Historic Data) for more details

- Even if a product was started and aborted and restarted later on, it may be useful to co-relate them to improve upon time. This can be maintained by keeping an ID (let's call it Soul ID) and any two items (products, resources...) can be related by Soul ID so that even after one of them is eliminated (is dead) and restarts (rebirth), they can still be co-related
- If the pre-sales team needs to provide the quote for a task, it's typical that they check with the subject matter experts (SMEs) for the estimate. Besides checking with SMEs, it's equally important to capture and analyze the historic patterns of how accurate have been our quotes for similar tasks in the past vs. actual money spent on their delivery
- Same goes for the risk i.e. the risk probability should be dynamic and tracked based upon how many of those risks have become a real issue in the past

Chapter 1.2.7 (Balance Productivity vs. Operational Overhead)

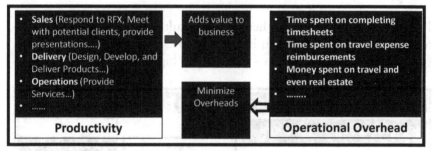

Fig 1.2.3 Productivity and Operational Overhead

We should minimize expenses on operational overhead

There's a difference between internal requirements (highlighted above in chapter 1.2.6 - Balance External vs. Internal Requirements) and operational overhead. Although neither of them are directly related to revenue or profitability, internal requirements provide a base to achieve overall profitability, whereas operational overhead is a pure wastage although necessary to some extent. Therefore, the operational overhead cost should be minimized to the extent required.

Here are some examples of Operational Overhead:

- Time spent on completing timesheets
- Time/Money spent on travel

- Time/Money spent to complete any governance/regulation issues although the knowledge is required to implement them
- Money spent on Real Estate
- Time spent on other types of formal paperwork

It might be effective to maintain a record of all money spent on various overheads with TCO costs/benefits and compare them with alternative approach – that can help.

As an example, if there are only 5 employees all working on independent projects and working in an office – is it proper to spend money on real estate or can they work from home?

Chapter 1.2.8 (Balance Bureaucracy vs. Flexibility)

In a bureaucratic system, we may follow processes blindly without realizing that some of the assumptions, market conditions and historic patterns have changed but they no longer provide intended business value

In a highly flexible system, there may be multiple processes/standards to follow that may create confusion and people may change the processes based upon personal interests – and provide bigger risk.

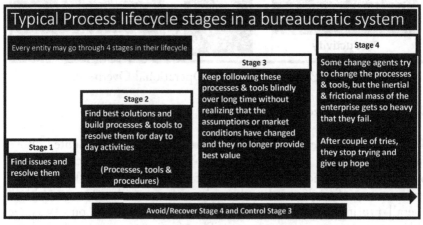

Fig 1.2.4 Process Lifecycle

We believe, each enterprise (where an enterprise may vary from an individual to a nation or even higher level) may go through 4 stages in life (shown in above diagram) i.e.

1. An enterprise encounters some problems/issues and creates solutions to resolve them. After going over same type of issues many times, they realize what are the best solutions

2. Once they find best solutions for common type of issues/problems, they formalize those solutions and convert them into recommended procedures/tools with processes and build rules where those tools/procedures/processes must be followed on day to day basis for all operational activities

3. Many times, these rules, processes, tools, and procedures are enforced blindly for a long time and even though the situations, market conditions, staffing requirements, company goals, and many other factors may have changed over time. They may no longer provide profitability and can be improved over time and proper changes should be made to those rules/processes/tools/procedures

4. Some change agents within the company realize the need for improvements. In some situations, and some companies, it may be easy to suggest and convince all leaders to make improvements, but practically may be difficult to implement those improvements. If those innovative change agents attempt to make improvements a few times but those don't get implemented, they stop trying again and again. That may be the worst situation since even the probability of suggesting improvements is minimized.

Highly bureaucratic businesses may be a bit too conservative, and even if some of the change agents can convince the leaders to change the processes and tools, it may be highly difficult to implement those changes. At the same time, having no processes especially in large business may have even more challenges since that will lack standardization, governance issues and can be misused. Ideally in a large and mature enterprise, we should have well defined processes but regularly review and change them based upon market conditions and historic patterns.

In smaller and newer businesses, having flexibility of processes is not a big challenge that allows to evaluate them and choose the best processes as they mature. However, even smaller businesses should have a proper balance as they mature.

Chapter 1.2.9 (Balance Outsourcing vs. Insourcing)

Outsourcing means using external resources (people) for getting any job done whereas Insourcing means using internal resources (people) within business to get the job done. Outsourcing may include Onshore or Offshore resources where Offshore refers to using resources from low-cost countries. Moreover, nearshore may refer to outsourcing (or offshore) but to a nearby country.

For any project/service, should we use internal or external resources, or a combination and how to decide their proper balancing based upon various tangible/intangible factors like:

Tangible factors to consider

- Staffing Cost: One of the easiest parameters i.e. what is the direct staffing cost of each resource. At times, companies use staffing cost as the only factor to think that offshore resources are much less expensive but one should consider all potential factors
- Direct Cost: Any additional costs related to insourcing resources (employees) like medical benefits, vacation, 401K contributions etc.
- Outsourcing management/admin team overhead: Additional overhead to maintain Outsourcing - this overhead may be even more when outsourcing is related to offshore assignments like ex-patriates. Ex-Patriates refers to internal employees who are sent to outsourcing (especially overseas to manage offshore outsourcing). Typically, for those ex-patriates, besides all expenses as employees, many additional expenses are involved when they work in another country.
- Training Related Cost: The overall training cost may be lesser if the individual stays with the business for a long time. Typically, effective training cost may be less for employees, more for insourcing contractors, and even more for outsourcing resources.
- Cost of infra-structure: In case of remote outsourcing (esp. offshore assignment), we may need to provide separate framework for infra-structure addressing access, security, and regulatory issues where there may be some restrictions of using overseas framework
- Maintenance Cost: Whereas infra-structure cost may include the capital expenses to set up the infra-structure, ongoing maintenance of infra-structure expenses may also vary
- Communication Usage Charges: Whereas infra-structure cost may include the capital expenses to set up communication link, ongoing operational communication expenses may also vary
- Travel Related Cost: If offshore resources are remotely located (esp. with onshore assignment), the travel costs may also vary

Intangible factors to consider

- Impact on the quality
  - ➤ Cost due to longer development time
  - ➤ Cost due to impact on product quality
  - ➤ Cost due to impact on dependent systems
  - ➤ Cost due to synchronization and longer link delay (latency) where products/services are delivered by multiple internal/external resources
- Cost associated with major risks (Opportunity & Threats)
  - ➤ Reusability of resources across critical Projects
  - ➤ Cost of bringing resources on board
  - ➤ Cost associated with attrition of resources
  - ➤ Long-term resource skill investment
  - ➤ Delayed time to market, if quality has impacts like longer development time, product quality, or impact of dependent system
  - ➤ Cost associated with Downsizing of staff i.e. if we keep internal resources but remove them later on, there's additional cost
  - ➤ Intellectual Property Leakage and their misuse

Finally, one should collect all parameters for a project (or tasks within a project), provide relative weightage of various factors as well as an algorithm to compute overall effective cost. Then provide various combinations and use the best combination based upon the least effective overall cost as a major factor.

Moreover, there are 3 main types of contact assignments for outsourcing i.e. **'Fixed Bids'**, **'Ongoing Operations/Services'**, and **'Time & Material'**

1. If a company uses offshore services to manufacture a product, typically they provide their requirements with quality control, pricing, and when they need that product i.e. more related to 'Fixed-Bid'. This way the company has lesser risk and they know the product will meet the quality, price and timing of delivery.
2. Even for ongoing operations/services (like Help Desk), the results are known immediately and therefore, the risk is very low
3. Many times, offshore assignments are signed based upon 'Time & Material' (especially for IT projects). Since the control over day to day operations is limited to offshore processing, the risk on when the product (especially software products) will be ready, and its quality is highly limited. So, it's important to balance the 'Fixed-Bid', 'Ongoing Operations/services', vs. 'Time & Material' assignment especially for Offshore projects.

Chapter 1.2.10 (Balance Project Management vs. People Management)

Main purpose of a project manager is to provide best value (short-term and one-time value for that project) for the project whereas a people manager has to consider the overall long-term, and ongoing value that may include employee/employer benefits.

If an individual is not contributing proper value to the project, a project manager's loyalty is towards the project and to provide short-term return on investment. Project Manager may take 3 steps i.e.

1) Inform the team member
2) Inform the people manager of the individual
3) Protect the project i.e. may replace the individual if needed

A people manager may need to go much further to optimize long-term return on investment. If an individual is not contributing expected short-term return for a project, people manager may need to evaluate - why and may need to reassign the individual to different project based upon various factors or provide some training to the individual.

Based upon PMI, the Functional organization may refer to situation where only people manager exists; Projectized organization where only project managers exist; Matrix organization is where both exist and actions can be balanced. This balancing may impact accordingly and same individual may serve two different activities. Refer to sub-section 3.3 for more details on (Project Management).

Chapter 1.2.11 (Balance Inter vs. Intra Project Collaboration)

Intra-project collaboration refers to collaboration of all tasks during entire lifecycle of a project/program, whereas inter-project collaboration refers to learning from similar tasks across different projects. A program can involve multiple projects, requiring inter-project collaboration.

Intra-project tasks include tasks across various phases such as sales, pursuit, requirements, design, implementation, testing, deployment, documentation, ongoing support...

An example of the tools/processes to maintain intra-project collaboration is a Requirements Traceability Matrix (RTM) that tracks what was required by the internal/external customer, and its accomplishments across various stages.

It's important to track relationships across different phases to ensure that we are acting based upon requirements i.e. provide what the customer needs and don't waste unnecessary effort on something not required, plus don't miss any requirements. Still learn from the experience and make it better and suggest/sell more requirements for the customer.

Many times, a business uses different RTM tools to track phase1 to phase2, phase2 to phase3 and so on, and there may be a challenge to synchronize the two tools and thus how to co-relate phase1 to phase3 properly? As an example, it may provide proper balancing between (say) requirements and design, and development and testing but we may not test all parts needed by the customer or might test more than what is needed – that may be an issue to the project output and cost

Inter-project collaboration includes comparing various projects and finding the best/most suitable actions as needed and learn/act accordingly across multiple dimensions like:

- **Knowledge sharing**: We should learn across multiple projects to find out what works best and use that as a base to use for future projects
- **Templates**: Re-use various artifacts and documents with common templates to maximize re-use and minimize expenses
- **Tools used**: What tools are used for which projects and use factual data as a base to find which tools work best for what kind of projects
- **Resources used**: which resources are best for what type of projects
- **Customers**: What are common/separate factors across various customers
- **Cultures**: What cultures to follow across various customers and other factors
- **Languages**: Which speaking and programming languages are important for common projects and who are best experts on those
- **Countries**: Common/separate factors across various countries
- ....

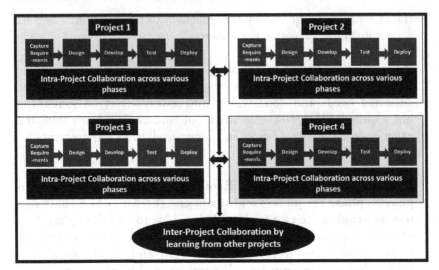

Fig 1.2.5 Overall Project Collaboration

Ideally, we should ensure complete collaboration for intra-project tasks across various phases, and utilize best input from other projects via inter-project collaboration for optimal value.

Chapter 1.2.12 (Balance Quality vs. Quantity)

Do you want to buy one great house for $900K or three houses of $300K each? Do you want to have one greatest talented child, two of average talents, or three with lower talent?

Quality vs. quantity may vary based upon the product/service as well, many other factors including buyer's mindset.

As a business owner, you may need to understand the buyer's approach and then decide whether to sell few high quality expensive cars or high volume less expensive cars.

Typically, high quality means high profit margins but less quantity, whereas high quantity means lower profit margins but more quantity.

Let's say, for CAR1 - we are selling only 100 cars with $10,000 profit/car; and for CAR2 – 1,000 cars with $1,000 profit/car. Total profit is $1M either way (100*10,000, or 1,000*1,000). CAR1 is better quality/less quantity whereas CAR2 is more quantity/lower quality.

Risks can vary i.e. if few customers walk out, the overall profitability is heavily impacted for high quality product i.e. if 50 customers walk out, our net profit for CAR1 goes down to $500K (50*10,000) and for CAR2 to $950K (950*1,000).

Similarly, if there's some impact on cost/sales per product, the risk can be higher for more quantity products i.e. if the cost goes up by $500, the net profitability for CAR1 would be $950K (100*9,500) and for CAR2, it will go down to $500K (1,000*500).

Chapter 1.2.13 (Balance Content vs. Formatting)

For any document, presentation, communication, dress style and other activities (especially facing the users) – What's more important i.e. what it contains (content) or how it looks (formatting)?

Perhaps both are important and should be balanced on many factors such as:

1. Who are the customers and their mindset?
2. Are these the initial activities, or periodic activities? Perhaps initial activities need better formatting and periodic activities may be more related to content although some portions of formatting (like user-friendliness) are equally important even for periodic activities
3. If the activities are related more for social relationships, formatting is more important whereas technical activities may be focused more on the content

Here are some activities that may need different balancing between content and formatting:

1. Any presentation, documents, user interface for the tools, web-sites i.e. their content and how they look should be balanced
2. If one buys a car, its style, branding, and other formatting activities may be equally important besides its price (TCO), quality and other content activities. Customers with less affordability normally concentrate more on the content than formatting or style or branding
3. What clothes you wear may depend to some extent on the content (i.e. must be able to take care of cold weather) but perhaps how it looks (formatting) may be more important

4. Various social activities like what parties you attend, people who want to socialize with, your image in the society may have higher priority for formatting

Regardless of the type of activity, it's important to balance the content and formatting for overall profitability considering all tangible and intangible factors.

Chapter 1.2.14 (Balance Perception vs. Reality)

When it comes to marketing, what customers think of a product/service is more important than what the product/service providers think based upon their definition of reality in terms of how great the product or service is - since unless it can be marketed, it can't achieve the profitability. This can also be termed as Subjective vs. Objective judgement.

If in a society, people's perception may be based on many factors including religion and/or culture, that may be an important factor in delivering the proper product. There are many other areas where it may be difficult to perform real computations to understand people's perception – such as politics, media, film industry, racism etc.

Data for such activities may be captured based upon historic data of people's perception and then the computational data can be balanced with the historic perception data. Another important input can be via customer surveys.

Chapter 1.2.15 (Balance As-Is vs. To-Be scenario)

Let's say the US president wanted US individual to land the moon back in 1960's.

Let's see what's required to land the US individual to moon from 5 major areas i.e.:

- **Technology**: We had to achieve a minimum speed of Escape Velocity (~25,000 miles/hour) which is the minimum speed needed for an object to "break free" from the gravitational attraction of earth
- **Business**: What do we need to accomplish from business perspective? That includes all financial aspects, partnerships etc.

needed (say need partnership with Soviet Union) to land on the moon?

- **Process**: What process will be needed to land on the moon?
- **Information**: What data and information will be needed and what kind of collaboration will be required to capture that data, analyze it and utilize it to land on the moon?
- **Organization**: What organizational structure and resources will be needed to land on the moon?

Next, we need to analyze the current scenario to understand where we are today compared to the to-be requirements from same major 5 areas i.e.:

- **Technology**: Let's say that current maximum speed is 5K miles/hour
- **Business**: No partnership with Soviet Union
- **Process**: Examine what processes are being used and how these are compatible with what's needed
- **Information**: Evaluate as to what data and information that will be needed, and what exists today
- **Organization**: Current organizational structure and resources

'Where we are' (As-Is or Existing Architecture) and 'Where we want to be' (To-Be or Reference/Target Architecture)?

First, we can utilize the best knowledge to define the best enterprise architecture (Reference Architecture) and then make it a bit more practical to build the target architecture.

Staying close to the space example, consider creating the solution components, preparing, launching, and finally walking on the moon.

Plan, Prepare, Create, do, achieve (image courtesy: NASA)

From rocket on the ground ... to => **Walk on the moon**

Fig 1.2.6 Solutioning Components

Once we understand where we are and where we want to be, we may need multiple phases for various areas and define complete roadmaps and how to collaborate them to optimize the outcome.

As an example, let's say - we can get 10K speed in 2nd year, 15K in 3rd year, 20K in 4th year, and finally escape velocity of 25K after a total of 5 years using 5 phases for technology. Similarly, what phases and how many are needed for each area. Finally, how to best collaborate across various areas and phases to reach the destination (moon in time) with lowest cost and best quality.

That balancing between where we are and where we need to reach and how to balance across various areas is very important for any delivery.

Chapter 1.2.16 (Balance Actions vs. Outcome)

What you do (aka '**Karma**' in Hindi) and what you achieve (aka '**Phal**' in Hindi) are highly related. Typically, outcome may depend upon tons of factors that are beyond your control and you can't even measure them or may not even be aware of many factors that may accomplish them.

If you cross the same road under similar situations regularly, it may suddenly result in an accident based upon other vehicles or various natural factors.

If you have no wrong intent, and you have taken the best decisions based upon the best data at that time, and used 100% of your capacity, you have performed the best you could.

Another way to look at success is based upon the outcomes. Although sometimes the outcome may be completely unexpected, that's the best you can do.

To balance the two, you should use the historic results as another major data input, combine it with any additional inputs related to predictions and forecast, and analyze these before taking next best action so that it is based on an informed decision.

Chapter 1.2.17 (Balance Passion vs. Practicality)

If you want to keep walking despite extreme friction and anti-movement factors and try to minimize the anti-forces, that's passion. Being passionate can be really great and may really serve as a major factor in achieving success.

If even after trying for a long time, your effective movement is still below expected value but your passion still forces you to continue walking, that's not practical. Based upon various factors, it may be worth and more practical to limit your passion.

Of course, it may depend upon various factors. If you are struck somewhere, where your life is in danger, you may continue your passion till your life threat is controlled. If you are struck on top of an extremely high mountain (say Mount Everest), in really bad weather without any apparent help, and you feel you are very likely to die, don't stop your passion to survive.

This balancing is very important when it comes to business. If you want to get into a new business that's related more to your passion than business profitability, you may need to balance the passion with practicality based upon various factors and their cost/benefit analysis.

It may be important to maintain data that will show net benefit over time and decide accordingly the degree of passion to maintain.

Chapter 1.2.18 (Balance Innovation vs. Reality)

Using top down approach with high-level vision may be innovative but theoretical with more risk and more reward. It can provide very high opportunity at low probability.

Bottom-up approach may be more realistic, may take long time to capture real data, limited return on investment (ROI) and may not include the wish-lists. Being realistic provides lower opportunity but with high probability since it's based more on real low-level facts.

Typically, top-down approach starts from top and stops in the middle with black boxes, bottom-up approach starts from bottom and stops in the middle.

One should build both top-down/bottom-up models, rationalize the two to provide proper balancing and then build a roadmap.

Top-Down approach is more related to innovation and creativity whereas bottom-up approach is more related to reality.

Being **Pro-active vs. Reactive** is like being Innovative vs. Realistic.

Being Innovative might provide higher opportunity but low probability and being Realistic may control high threats and provide stable profitability. Being reactive may provide more of short-term profitability at low risk whereas being pro-active may provide more long-term profitability at high risk.

In short, provide proper balancing between Innovation & Reality.

Chapter 1.2.19 (Balance Crazy vs. Non-crazy workers)

Sometimes there's less work and sometime there's more work. However, typically same set of people perform more work since the reward of doing great work is more work. Those people, however, work on the expectancy theory and typically have high energy, ideas and capacity and it's for the management to ensure that they don't burn out.

For long-term benefit, employee's professional vs. personal life also need to be balanced and again the management should try to accomplish that the crazy employees try to achieve their personal life accomplishments besides professional accomplishments.

Chapter 1.2.20 (Balance Local vs. Remote employee assignments)

For many of consulting companies, at times when a new project starts, they assign an individual who may be on bench but not local; although there may a fully compatible local person available on bench.

Keeping local employees for local projects can help the employee, employer, and the client.

Chapter 1.2.21 (Balance under pressure vs. not under pressure)

Working under pressure can serve as a positive catalyst by double checking the results and exploring various solutions.

If there's pressure on a regular basis, it may serve as a negative catalyst and people may stop even looking at a single solution. Moreover, consistent pressure can also ignore a real emergency need and people may not care for an urgency to act as they would consider it as a routine.

Chapter 1.2.22 (Balance Similar vs. different team opinions/ approach)

As long as various members of the same team including managers have the same vision/mission, different opinions/approach may serve as a positive catalyst and confrontation may be a good mechanism to review all approaches and select the best one.

However, if the same team members continue having different opinions, it might impact their team co-ordination and may take long time to continue resolving different opinions. A great leader can have the charisma to transform the power of conflicts to a synergy of tapping different points of view to supplement and strengthen the existing and drive collaboration when they lead by example with an intention to create a better world.

Chapter 1.2.23 (Balance working independently vs. with team)

Should all individuals be working on various activities as a team or independently? Both have pros/cons.

If everyone works independently throughout the project, we lack collaboration to monitor what we are doing, any changes, or learn from each other.

If we always work as a team, the efficiency of low-level tasks may be reduced.

Ideally working independently or as a team should be properly balanced. Start as a team, define all activities with overall collaboration and task assignments. Once the tasks are assigned to individuals (or smaller teams), let them start independently (or in small groups). Once the tasks are complete, again restart as a team.

Moreover, periodically work as a team to monitor the performance, status, requirement changes, design changes, data collection, and learn from each other.

Chapter 1.2.24 (Balance across multiple Domains)

All major issues in a business may have problems across multiple domains.

There are multiple domains within a business and many of the domains are a bit easier to predict, simulate, and then act accordingly. Some of the domains that are more difficult to anticipate include: Economic domain and Mindset Paradigm Shift.

Here are some of the domains:

- **Technical**: This may be one of the easiest domain to simulate - the industry is already well stable in majority of technology advancements
- **Financial**: The goals are well defined and easy to simulate and act accordingly
- **Social**: Follow the social rules and act accordingly
- **Religious**: Follow the religious rules and act accordingly
- **Political**: Follow the political rules and act accordingly
- **Economic**: Perhaps difficult to predict and act accordingly
- ..
- **Mindset Paradigm Shift**: Perhaps the most difficult part and the main concern of this chapter is the mindset paradigm shift. Individual's mindset become more static and biased over time and if needed, more difficult to change.

    If people are more concerned with local spreadsheets for maintaining data, it becomes a challenge to change that mindset although this can be a big concern for collecting/collaborating factual metrics.

If people are more concerned with male-dominated society, it takes a while to change that mindset.

If business mindset is based on leadership by the number of years of experience and less dependent upon their outcome, that may be a challenge.

There can be many other examples of mindset paradigm shift such as admitting that the earth is round... But how to make it a bit easier to change the mindset?

Perhaps, best way could be to have periodic meetings and collect real data as a base and use that data as a demo to show the impact of various mindsets and try to make small adjustments on a periodic basis. That would make a bit easier to provide a mindset paradigm shift over time as needed.

Chapter 1.2.25 (Leader vs. Manager)

It's important to plan Strategic Balancing as a Leader, and implement them as a manager.

Leader	Manager
• Asks what and why	• Plans how and when
• Does the correct thing	• Does things correctly
• Takes the necessary risks	• Is risk cautious
• Long-range perspective	• Short-range perspective
• Challenges the status quo	• Accepts the status quo
• Plans strategy	• Plans tactics
• Sets the policy	• Sets standard operating procedures
• Seeks change	• Seeks continuity
• Develops vision & strategies	• Develops plans, budgets, & detailed steps
• Focuses on goals of innovation	• Focuses on goals for improvement
• Provides vision and persuasion	• Provides technology and administration
• Originates for managers to follow	• Imitates others
• Uses "transformational" communication	• Uses "transactional" communication
• Sets standards of excellence	• Sets standards of performance

Fig 1.2.7 Leaders versus Managers

There could be many more areas that need to be properly balanced to accomplish your goals.

Sub-Section 1.3

Improve over time

This sub section highlights how to learn and improve over time

Chapter 1.3.1 (Ensure quantitative improvements over time)

During various stages of any delivery, can we quantitatively verify that we are moving in the positive direction as per project requirements?

Keep a record of all delivery data results and use that as a base to check whether/not we are making improvements over time. If we complete a task in 100 hours last time, are we completing the same task in less than 100 hours next time? If not try to rationalize why not?

There is another example provided for testing/mock runs under Chapter 2.2.9 (Data Migration Quality)

Chapter 1.3.2 (Continual Tool Improvements)

How to properly select tools, regularly review them, and change them based upon market conditions and historic patterns?

If we are using multiple tools for maintaining relationship between various phases (like Requirements Traceability Matrix with main issue shown in chapter 1.2.11 (Balance Inter vs. Intra Project Collaboration) and it becomes difficult to co-relate those tools, is it justifiable to find a way to improve those tools so that Testing can be properly done based upon user requirements (as an example)?

If we have a very large volume, velocity, and variety of data that may be unstructured, should we use a Big Data tool?

If the data is distributed with suppliers and consumers at multiple locations, should we use the data on cloud? Depending upon the data security needs, should we use private cloud?

If we are using an extremely old tool, will it be difficult to maintain it based upon resource availability - if there are only few users of the old tool and that too for a limited period, it is worth spending much effort to improve that tool?

There could be many more examples, but it's important to monitor what tools are available, keep track of what tools we are using and their performance.

It can go both ways i.e. sometimes, it makes sense to improve the tools, but if the usage is not critical and highly limited and very expensive to upgrade the tool, should we upgrade that tool? That's where Cost/Benefit analysis would help.

Chapter 1.3.3 (Continual Process Improvements)

How to well define processes, regularly review them, and change them based upon market conditions and historic patterns?

Besides the tools, process improvements are equally important.

As an example, if we provide employee performance evaluation based upon capturing of performance data and feedback from their managers just towards end of fiscal year, is that good enough? It may have few issues like:

- The employee has a new people/project manager who doesn't know much about the employee
- The employee's performance has been completely different for the projects in the beginning of the project and end of fiscal year
- Employee performance evaluation process may take a good amount of time and that may have impact on other activities towards the end of the fiscal year

Perhaps, it might be better to improve the process to capture performance feedback from multiple people all around the year and still provide the impact to employees on a periodic basis. That may help on many issues i.e.

- People/Project Managers, and even colleagues can provide employee feedback on a regular basis
- Some feedback may be optional and some mandatory as needed
- Each type of feedback may have customizable relative weightage
- Not only current fiscal year data but even historic data should be maintained
- Last few days/months are not terribly busy for review

- Performance Evaluation can be more realistic and consistent across teams
- Who can access what data (including employees) can be customized
- Easy to learn from the experience using complete data both for employees and employers

Another example could be marketing/sales with least unnecessary overhead based upon factual data; improvement of tools/resources including cloud/big data/others that add value.

Besides these, there can be tons of other processes based upon their importance and available time and resources. Important processes should monitor and track on a regular basis and improve based on their cost/benefit analysis.

Sub-Section 1.4

Summary of Strategic Balancing

Key take away	How Strategic Balancing can help	Potential Leadership, Business, and/or Technical Framework Needed
1.2.1 Balance Sales vs. Delivery		
Promise based upon real capability	Minimize project abortion in the middle	Maintain proper cloud-based database and tools to track capabilities and their outcome
Sales/delivery pricing based upon factual data	We can win the deals by avoiding overquoting and minimize project loss by avoiding underquoting	Co-relate sales/delivery and capture actual pricing with Database-as-a-Service accessible from anywhere with security at any time through a user-friendly web interface
Risks based upon real issues	If the expected risk probability is based upon how often that became an issue, the risk related pricing of the contact can be more realistic	Use proper risk analysis tools by capturing all risks with their expected level of probability and how often they became real issues
1.2.2 Balance Market Side vs. Supply Side		
Sell a product/service based upon customer or business needs (Go to Market)	Minimize wastage by building products/services that can't be sold properly	Proper marketing tools based upon market research
Price a product/service based upon how much a customer is willing to pay and our delivery cost (Market Dynamics)	Minimize wastage by selling at a high price that's difficult to sell or at a lower price that can't achieve profitability	Use customer survey, competitor's pricing, and delivery pricing data as a base for future pricing

Key take away	How Strategic Balancing can help	Potential Leadership, Business, and/or Technical Framework Needed
Be more realistic for sales (Point of View)	High profitability based upon how realistic our promises have been over time	Use proper data prescriptive analytics tools to improve actions over time

1.2.3 Balance Existing Clients vs. Attracting New Customers

When competitors attract new customers, how to avoid losing existing customers (customer churns)?	Balancing by special deals to attract both existing/ new customers is equally important and losing existing customer may be even more expensive	KYC (Know your customer) database, feeds from social media (tweets, Facebook, linked-in) in near-real time (big data), look/ book feeds from third party as-a-service providers (viz. Adobe Audience Manager)
Lack of access to accurate information about customers' tastes, preferences, needs, can lead to churn	A central repository of all customer data that provides a 360° view of the customer; integration with social media, ability to access browsing history to understand customer concerns, pain points, and next best action to address discontent	

1.2.4 Balance Productivity vs. Profitability

Control project initiation to maximize value generation and effective profitability by minimizing the probability of aborting the project before completion?	Minimize initiating projects that have to be aborted in the middle	• Buy-In from leadership • Understand Client Needs • Framework to control Scope Creep • Resource Availability • Proper communication framework • Ensure proper Project-Mix • Delivery based upon client's satisfaction

Key take away	How Strategic Balancing can help	Potential Leadership, Business, and/or Technical Framework Needed
1.2.5 Balance Short-term vs. Long-term goals		
Keep making profit but plan to make profit in future as well	Ensure operational profits and profit for upcoming products/services	Money Tracking tools plus future planning tools
1.2.6 Balance External vs. Internal Requirements		
Keep internal requirements to capture internal real data as a base to provide external needs	High Profitability based upon actual results of sales/delivery	Tools to capture data on a Cloud and use it as Database-as-a-Service accessible from anywhere with security at any time through a user-friendly web interface
1.2.7 Balance Productivity vs. Operational Overhead		
Minimize Operational Overheads	High Profitability by reducing money wastage	Use proper tools/training to minimize operational costs like completing timesheets, travel expenses etc.
1.2.8 Balance Bureaucracy vs. Flexibility		
Use processes and procedures for operations but periodically update them based upon market conditions and historic patterns	Minimize overhead and maximize quality	Process Improvement Tools
1.2.9 Balance Outsourcing vs. Insourcing		
Ensure outsourcing (esp. offshore outsourcing) is profitable	High Profitability for the business	Outsource Tracking/Analyzing Tools for all types of business including ('Fixed Bids', 'Services', and Time & Material') where 'Time & Material' may be quite risky for offshore business

Key take away	How Strategic Balancing can help	Potential Leadership, Business, and/or Technical Framework Needed
1.2.10 Balance Project Management vs. People Management		
Maximize Project profitability as a project manager and overall people utilization as a people manager	Win-Win ratio for employer/employees	Use proper Project Management/People Management Tools
1.2.11 Balance Inter vs. Intra Project Collaboration		
Ensure full lifecycle integration of any deal and use that knowledge for other related deals	Optimizes delivery of a project and learn from other related projects	Use proper project/ portfolio management tools
1.2.12 Balance Quality vs. Quantity		
Optimize the quality of the outcome and how much to produce/sell	High Profitability	Use proper Quality/ Quantity control tools
1.2.13 Balance Content vs. Formatting		
Use proper means to communicate besides the content	Optimize customer satisfaction	Use Proper Communication Tools including customer surveys
1.2.14 Balance Perception vs. Reality		
Besides providing proper outcome, ensure customers view them as proper products/services	Optimize customer satisfaction	Use Customer Survey Tools
1.2.15 Balance As-Is vs. To-Be scenario		
Provide proper balancing for various phases across multiple areas based upon how to reach destination from where we are	Best overall Project Management	Use proper target/ existing architecture evaluation and project management tools to accomplish them via proper collaboration

Key take away	How Strategic Balancing can help	Potential Leadership, Business, and/or Technical Framework Needed
1.2.16 Balance Actions vs. Outcome		
Use proper actions based upon desired outcome and historic data	More realistic outcome	Use proper actual data and best tools to achieve the results – where you can control the actions
1.2.17 Balance Passion vs. Practicality		
Be passionate but be practical over time	More realistic outcome	Use actual data and proper tools to achieve probability and minimize impact by continuing with same passion for a long time. If you want to keep walking despite extreme friction and anti-movement factors and try to minimize the anti-forces, that's passion. Being passionate can be really great and may really serve as a major factor in achieving success. If even after trying for a long time, your effective movement is still below expected value but your passion still forces you to continue walking, that's not practical. Based upon various factors, it may be worth and more practical to limit your passion.
1.2.18 Balance Innovation vs. Reality		
Don't blindly implement patents or innovative ideas	High profitability	Use proper market research tools
1.2.19 Balance Crazy vs. Non-crazy workers		
Be more practical to manage crazy workers	Get more practical outcome from great resources	Use proper people management tools

Key take away	How Strategic Balancing can help	Potential Leadership, Business, and/or Technical Framework Needed
1.2.20 Balance Local vs. Remote employee assignments		
Use local resources to best extent	Win-Win situation for employer, clients, and staffing	Use proper project/ resource assignment tools. Many of consulting companies, at times when a new project starts, they assign an individual who may be on bench but not local; although there may a fully compatible local person available on bench. Keeping local employees for local projects can help the employee, employer, and the client
1.2.21 Balance under pressure vs. no pressure		
Don't use emergency unless really needed	Keep emergency useful when needed	Use proper tools to evaluate pressure
1.2.22 Balance Similar vs. different team opinions/approach		
Optimize different opinions as long as mission is common	Best way to accomplish the goal	Use proper tools to balance different ways of implementation
1.2.23 Balance working independently vs. with team		
Optimize team/individual contributions	High profitability	Use proper tools to check proper balancing needs
1.2.24 Balance across multiple Domains		
Balance mindset paradigm shift as needed	Perhaps most difficult accomplishment is to change people's mindset	Use proper periodic presentations to balance mindset as needed
1.2.25 Balance across Leadership vs. Management		
Optimize what to do and then get it done	Maximize profitability and minimize frustration	Use proper resources as leaders and as managers

SECTION 2

Technical Framework

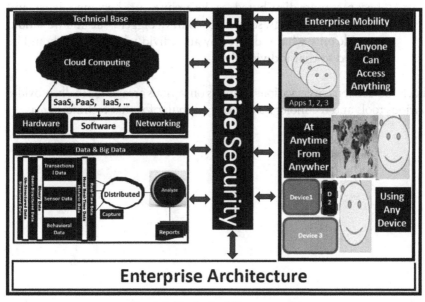

Fig 2.0 Technical Framework

This section provides basic understanding/framework of various technical areas

Main purpose of the book for Section 1 is to understand business mission, collaborate across various areas, collect all relevant data across those areas (current and historic), and perform proper cost/benefit analysis to optimize various areas to achieve the business mission. But to get down to details of various sub-sections and chapters within section 1, there is a need to understand the technical details at the conceptual level. This section covers those details under five major sub sections i.e.:

1. **Technical Base** - Includes all hardware, infrastructure, cloud computing, virtualization, IoT, Networking, and Base Software (Software, Architecture)
2. **Data and Big Data** - Data Engineering, Transactional Database, Data Warehouse, ETL Process (Extraction, Transformation, and

Loading), Business Intelligence, Data Mining, Big Data, Business Analytics i.e. how to collect data and convert to information

3. **Enterprise Architecture** – How to build a technical framework that can optimize the usage of various technical resources
4. **Enterprise Mobility** – How to allow anyone to access any part of the technology, using any device, from anywhere, and at any time
5. **Enterprise Security** - As the technical base expands, as the data becomes more distributed, as the architecture becomes bigger, and as mobility expands, security becomes a bigger issue and we should provide only what is desired by an individual plus what should be allowed to that individual

Each sub-section covers various chapters on various areas and finally provides various tools and technologies currently popular for that technical area.

Sub Section 2.1

Technical Base

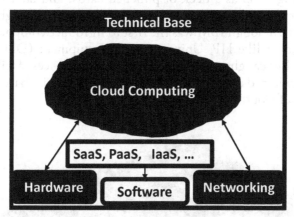

Fig 2.1 Technical Base

Computer systems are often segregated in three categories i.e. hardware, software, and supporting networks. Though boundaries are gradually blurring as more and more software is merging with hardware to drive superior performance and task specific optimization to leverage native couplings, these three broad categories are still the widely-used industry norm to segregate computer systems. Computer Systems also include Firmware that contains pre-populated software in hardware.

A human being is a good example of computer system. All parts of human body are the hardware and as we learn more and more that's part of our software. Even the hardware (when we are born) comes with genetic properties which is like the firmware. Just like a computer has a CPU with many components including peripherals, a human's brain serves as the CPU with eyes, ears, nose, hands, legs etc. as its peripherals. Just like the computer peripherals can work in parallel with CPU control. Human peripherals also work independently with control and messaging over brain. Moreover, all humans have strong networking between them.

Chapter 2.1.1. Hardware

Machine Circuit Boards, Electronics, and associated peripheral equipment's are often collectively termed hardware. When the cost of computers to begin with was significant, the norm was that you buy the hardware and software comes with it. In the early days, there were mainframe computers that fit in huge machine rooms and the users went to use the computing services at the installation facility by submitting a job as a deck of punched cards, and later by logging in to terminals connected directly to the computer through terminal concentrators. Though IBM was the first to introduce computing, many industry players like HP, Univac, Digital Equipment (DEC), Sperry, Fujitsu quickly caught on to offer comparable devices, facilities, and services. Modern day term often used for hardware is 'bare metal,' in the context of cloud.

Fig 2.1.1 A PC mother board (image courtesy: Pixabay)

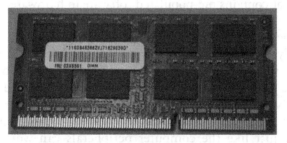

Fig 2.1.2 A memory card

The basic building block for all computing devices is a NAND Gate – (Not of AND), or a NOR (Not of OR) since these NAND and NOR gates have the functional completeness of all logic systems, which is accomplished by simple p-n junctions within a silicon wafer. A multitude of these compacted within the silicon wafer chip enables higher computing power. These NAND/NOR gates become the grass-root level processors that finally execute complex logic by way of breaking it all down to a level of steps that are simple enough to execute at the lowest level. From large scale integration to very large-scale integration (VLSI) to ultra-scale integration (USI), successive revolutions in compacting the computing capability have led to an Intel Pentium, Celeron, and now Corei7 chips boasting higher computing power, which is an order of magnitude more powerful than the original Mainframe. The mainframes have also evolved from earlier proprietary systems to now more open source compliant operating systems (viz. IBM 'Z' series on Linux) and modular, scalable architectures.

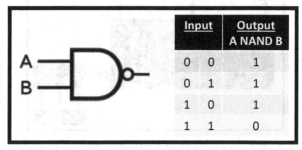

Fig 2.1.3 NAND gate and truth table

As VLSI (Very Large-Scale Integration) techniques matured, affordable larger computing power became available on smaller chips. Typically, once a patent expires, the technology matures and the scale tips from cutting edge to commodity. Moreover, the gates open for anyone who can develop and deliver it cheaper, faster, and better. A positive outcome of this trend is affordable cost and transitioning of manufacturing and development to off-shore that can help build the economy and strengthen interdependence among communities and nations of the world.

The scale of integration over time from 1970s through now has nearly followed Moore's law, doubling the number of transistors accommodated on a chip 'every year and a half' to 'two years'.

Chapter 2.1.2. Infrastructure

Term 'infrastructure' often includes hardware, but encompasses operating system platform, network, logical partitions of servers (LPARs), databases, storage devices, memory, printers, and others - that make computing, processing, job execution, and communication, a potential possibility. In today's environment-aware and power consumption conscious society, co-locating infrastructure and providing access using networking is a way to bring down the total cost of ownership. This approach enables redundancy of high-availability operations with low possibility of disaster recovery.

The term 'platform' often refers to an aspect of the infrastructure viz. hardware, OS (Operating System), database etc., like Oracle 12c is the database platform, or p570 (IBM p-series) is the hardware platform, or Linux is the OS platform.

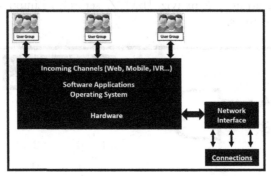

Fig 2.1.4 A conceptual view of hardware, software, and network

The term 'environment' often refers to specific set of computing resources and infrastructure provided for a specific phase of a project – development, test, staging, pre-production, UAT (User Acceptance Testing), production etc. Sometimes these phases can be combined to a single environment, like development and testing sliced over periods of time on the same environment to save on the cost of provisioning infrastructure. Different environments may also be accommodated on the same system by creating LPARs (logical partitions), depending on size and scaling of the hardware required.

HADR concepts:

High Availability (HA) is expressed like 99.9x %, implying uptime of an infrastructure environment, or collection as computing resources. With addition of each .x9, there are stringent mandatory requirements, like moving the stand-by system to over 1200 miles away, if an unforeseen flood, fire, or riots may destroy a system infrastructure in a specific town, state, or country. Since higher availability infrastructures are often very expensive, most non-critical applications settle for Disaster Recovery (DR) that meet specified time (usually a few hours, or by next day SLAs) to bring up an alternate infrastructure and recover from backed up data for business continuity. Load sharing/balancing and high-availability go hand-in glove, leveraging the infrastructures to meet the peek loads while settling for limited downgrading of performance (viz. response time) in the events of failure or disaster.

With the advent of cloud, it is increasingly becoming affordable to provision DR and HA as data can be backed up on network storage with built in redundancy, servers can be brought up on demand, and loads can be balanced and shared among clusters.

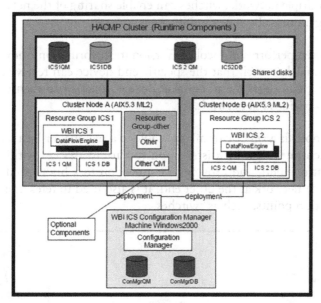

Fig 2.1.5 HA fail over of resource group

Chapter 2.1.3. Network

Network is the connection between two or more devices. These devices can be hand held smart phones, tablets, laptops, mainframe computers, routers, switches, and nodes. From local to wide area networks to wi-fi, the term network has come to imply 'connectivity' that enables a device or multiple devices to establish a connection to access or send data to and from other device or devices. Many use the terms network, internet, and connection interchangeably, though each one of these has its own specific scope.

The major components in a network solution are modems, switches, routers, multiplexers, and media over which the signal is transmitted – satellite, microwave, UHF, VF, HF (radio), fiber optic, coaxial or copper cables, and power line carrier communication are common example of transmission media.

Modems perform modulation and de-modulation that varies the amplitude, frequency, or phase of a base signal in accordance with the data or speech that is intended to be transmitted.

Network switches route the data packets (which can include voice encoded as data) from source to destination by deciphering destination address contained in header of the data packet and routing it to the appropriate circuit. Multiple network switches can enable sharing of the network load by routing among alternate circuit routes.

Routers often perform protocol conversion (transformation from one data format to another, such that the specific end device can receive data in a form that it can digest), and connect devices together to each-other and to a local or wide area network.

Network node is a generic term applicable to a regional or local end-point that concentrates data for distribution to various devices within a local segment at one end, and provides a connection to a high-speed regional or wide area network at the other end. It is also used to refer intermediate redistribution points, such as switches.

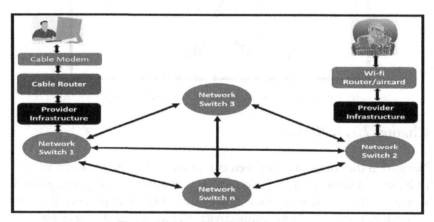

Fig 2.1.6 User/Device Connection
(connected to a modem, router, modem, network switch, and circuit components to communicate with another end device user)

Chapter 2.1.4. Software

Software is a term used to define all sorts of programs, utilities, tools, and applications that enable the execution of a given task using computing resources. One may write a program to count a set of numbers, write a middleware utility that performs routing and mediation of messages across diverse systems, or create an operating system that is supported on a set of hardware platforms. The generic term can refer to a lot of options and an interpretation is specific to the context of what that software would achieve as functionality.

System software is a bundle of operating system, tools and utilities that enable the applications to run on a specific hardware platform. Application software achieves very specific functionality. For instance, Microsoft Word is a word processing software, and part of MS Office suite of application programs.

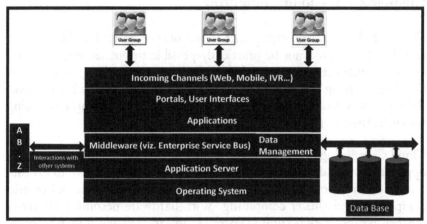

Fig 2.1.7 Software Stack
(Ranging from operating system to middleware applications to portal)

Traditional way of having an army of programmers on site to develop specific set of programs is gradually giving way to off-site and off-shore models in view of cost pressures. In order to achieve meaningful results, a minimal on-site presence of a few coordinating and business analyst team members is essential to understand client needs and communicate these to the larger off-site design and development team. Live meetings and online collaboration tools are now making seamless working between geographically dispersed teams possible.

Application Programming Interfaces (APIs) are now ubiquitous and allow various teams to access the development environments from anywhere, and the advent of Microservices now makes it possible to deploy code, test, move to production and support (DevOps) leveraging the cloud.

What emerged as an inter-network of networks (internet) has now become synonym with the web, bringing ease to create and deploy websites and customize content on the fly. Freebie tools like Wordpress now bring this power and ability to anyone with access to the network and an inclination to do something creative. Even a non-hands-on CEO can self-learn, create and deploy a beginner's website in less than an hour, and keep revising and updating as time permits. It is nothing short of a miracle that the number of websites worldwide has grown from the first site launched on August 6, 1991 to over 1.2bn in May 2017. This growth is here to stay, and likely to gain even further momentum. The gap between world population and the number of internet users is also fast diminishing.

Chapter 2.1.5. Cloud Computing

Think of cloud as something that is not on the ground sitting next to you. While it would not be practically possible to put servers, software, and other infrastructure several thousand feet above the ground unless there was a flying platform or a tethered balloon that would house them, the term *cloud* in the context of computing has come to imply accessing resources from *anywhere*.

Cloud Computing is a more recent paradigm that can be visualized as the opposite of early day users flocking to the computing facility to execute a job. It brings together and builds on the traditional concepts of grid computing, and cluster computing. With hardware becoming relatively inexpensive, network becoming faster, secure, and reliable, it now becomes possible to place a cluster of computing resources anywhere on the planet at a place that can be securely connected through a high-speed network, and make these resources available to users who need them, on-demand. This bundle of computing resources that can be provisioned and made available on-demand from anywhere connectivity exists, is notionally referred to as the 'cloud.' All you need at the front-end is basically any device that supports a thin client like a smart phone, a tablet, laptop, desktop etc. Once you are on the network, you can get access to the computing resources on-demand.

While Grid computing comprises many computers working together to achieve one goal, cloud computing is aimed to provide any type of computing resource for independent tasks. Grid computing is a form of distributed computing and parallel computing, and divides a single large task among many loosely coupled computers.

Cloud computing is about virtualizing the entire IT stack, from infrastructure to application services, including computing power and make it available as a priced utility. Grid and cluster computing primarily address the problem of efficiently executing large computations. Cloud computing is about making any IT resource ubiquitous, accessible from anywhere and at any time.

A computer cluster is a group of linked computers, working together closely to form the equivalent of a single computer. The components of a cluster are commonly connected through fast local area networks.

Compute clusters are a Single System concept - collection of nodes in the cluster collectively acting as a single system, implying single root, single file system etc. Single nodes are homogeneous in nature, so addition of new nodes or replacement of those shutting down is transparent. The cloud concept is very similar as collection of resources, and "virtual" computing clusters can be requested on-demand from providers, leveraging a large distributed network of nodes to provide resources.

Users of cloud based services are neither concerned, nor need to be aware of the underlying architecture, topology and other design details of the cloud provisioning. They are, however, concerned about the service level agreements (SLAs) being met – like response time, and the resources being provisioned as needed, and being released after usage. Thus, compute clusters are the basis of a cloud computing infrastructure and "virtual" clusters can be requested on demand.

-aaS

The term 'as-a-Service' (-aaS) is often used to define the specific provisioning that is being sought through the cloud. The major categories in this space are SaaS, PaaS, IaaS, QaaS, BPaaS, DBaaS, referring to Software, Platform, Infrastructure, Quality, Business Processes, and Database, respectively, as a Service that are provisioned through the cloud, as needed. What it implies is that in any combination, these items can be provisioned, almost like a-la-carte where you as the end customer and user/consumer can decide as to what exactly you want and specify that by picking choices from the menu (typically a cloud services catalog using a self-service web portal), or arrange with the service provider to provision what is required. Often you would be able to leverage flexibility offered by the cloud to optimize resources and lower the total cost of ownership by scaling up or down, provisioning higher capacities when needed, and down-sizing when your peak loads are met.

The 'cloud' paradigm offers great benefits like charging the clients only for what they use and how much they use, shifting their capital expenses (capex) to operating expenses (opex), lowering the total cost of ownership and leveraging resources from anywhere, including the design, development, test, and operation teams, besides the software and hardware infrastructure.

On the flip side, security and speed have been the two major concerns for 'cloud' provisioned services, as clients are concerned about someone else sharing the same infrastructure and resources as them, and the latency introduced through access over the network of what otherwise could be next door. Both concerns are being addressed, and service providers are increasingly moving towards providing more secure and faster services through the cloud.

One can expect that while both security and response time/speed of access would continue to be concerns for several years to come for most cloud based services, improvement is on the way as these are being continually addressed through international awareness and maturing industry cooperation to promote higher standards and compliance thereof.

Various concepts in cloud computing:

Virtualization refers to infrastructure being shared between many computing resources like physical servers or application servers, providing more efficient utilization of IT resources and lower hardware cost through resource consolidation and economies-of-scale. Resources are dynamically provisioned (or de-provisioned) based on consumer demands.

Elasticity refers to scaling IT environments up or down by any magnitude as needed to satisfy customer demands, optimizing resource utilization and increasing flexibility. A user can create, launch, and terminate server instances as needed, and pay accordingly. Cloud bursting refers to automatically adding and subtracting capacity. Elasticity enables handling of the sudden, unexpected workloads.

Scalability refers to planned level of capacity and overhead, providing leverage for up-resourcing, as anticipated and needed.

Automation is the key to infrastructure management for cloud computing as it helps to reduce the cost and provides standardization for deployment and management of IT services by eliminating errors caused through manual procedures and processes. Microservices and DevOps are key concepts to execute automation in this regard.

Provisioning is the automated creating, preparing, and configuring computing resources like physical servers, operating system, middleware, and application server, network, storage space, services, etc. With pattern-based provisioning, different software components needed to support a given task are provisioned and integrated in a single logical step to address specific needs like high availability, security, or scalability.

Deprovisioning is the automated restoration of computing resources to their respective resource pools like physical servers, operating system, middleware and application server, network, storage space, services, etc.

Public cloud refers to computing resources shared by multiple tenants. It is for open use by the public. Hardware, application, and bandwidth costs are covered by the provider. The offerings are 'as is' services. Users pay for usage on as-needed model. Since services are offered over an open public network, typically there are security concerns, especially when computing to be performed involves processing data of a sensitive nature, like personal identifiable information, critical business data that can pose risk if leaked to competitors, related to defense etc.

Private cloud is typically owned by an enterprise to cater resources for multiple lines of business or departments, or alternately a cloud service provider offering dedicated or shared solution for multiple tenants. The private cloud can only be accessed by internal users, mitigating the security concerns of a public cloud to a large extent. For shared private clouds, isolation of tenants is achieved through security zone assignment and dedicated networks. Dedicated private clouds can either be deployed on-premise or off-premise, while shared private clouds are typically deployed as off-premise.

Hybrid cloud model is a combination of two or more cloud types (viz. private, public, community) brought together through data and application integration, and can enable substantial savings in service delivery and management through resources provided via the public cloud. Business enterprises leverage this model flexibly in situations where not so sensitive data can be processed through public cloud computing resources while reserving private cloud computing resources for data that is of a more sensitive or critical nature. Since applications and analytics would require access to both - robust security, integration, and firewalls are enabled to ensure seamless flow of data over the fence across public and private clouds.

Private	Managed Private	Hybrid Private	Community	Public
• Enterprise Owned Data Center/s	• 3rd Party Operated Data Center/s	• 3rd Party Hosted and Operated	• Shared Cloud services among enterprises	• Shared among various users
• Scalability • Automatic • Provisioning • Chargeback • Virtualization • Security • Performance • Ownership • Capital Expenses	• Scalability • Automatic • Provisioning • Chargeback • Virtualization • Security • Performance • Operational Expenses	• Internal & External Services • Integrated Provisioning based on requirements • Business Needs for security • Data Privacy • Latency concerns • Medium Control	• Better Security control than Public need based provisioning	• Multi-tenancy • Scalability • Automatic provisioning • Standardized Offerings • Consumption-based pricing
• Highest Exit Cost	• Medium to High Exit Cost	• Medium Exit Cost	• Low Exit Cost	• Lowest Exit Cost
Highest Control	High Control	Medium Control	Low Control	Lowest Control

Fig 2.1.8 (Table): public, private, and hybrid cloud characteristics

Software as a Service refers to use of the provider's applications running on the cloud. The applications are accessible from devices through a thin client interface, such as a web browser, or a program interface. The consumer does not control the underlying cloud infrastructure or application capabilities, except user-specific application configuration settings. Examples of SaaS are Google docs and Salesforce.com.

Platform as a Service refers to deployment on the cloud infrastructure of consumer-created or acquired applications using programming languages, libraries, services, and tools provided and supported by the provider. The consumer does not manage the underlying cloud infrastructure, but controls the deployed applications and associated configuration settings. The computing platform describes hardware architecture and application framework that allows software to run.

Infrastructure as a Service refers to provisioning of processing, storage, networking, and computing resources, enabling the consumers to deploy and run required software, which can include operating systems and applications. The consumer does not manage the underlying cloud infrastructure, but has control over operating systems, storage, and deployed applications; and some control of networking components like host firewalls. Examples of IaaS are Amazon Elastic Compute Cloud, CenturyLink, and Soft-Layer.

Database-as-a-Service is managed by a cloud provider (public or private) to support consumer applications, without the consumer application team assuming traditional responsibility for database administration. Users can typically run databases on the cloud independently, using a virtual image, or purchase access to a database service. SQL and NoSQL databases are currently available. DBaaS can offset costs related to keeping data locally, archive, backup, and recovery. Examples include Cloudera, dashDB, Cloudant/CouchDB, MongoDB, Amazon DynamoDB, and Apache Cassandra.

Here's an analogy for the cloud. Within a family, all close relatives can be clustered to share their services and since they are well related, security is not a big issue. We might like to relate and share across other families via grid computing and control the sharing to avoid any misuse. We might acquire some common home service providers for shared services, some common time-shared hotels and other services just like cloud computing. As kids are very young, family provides almost full service and kids just make use of those services (like SaaS), as kids grow, they manage more services as they grow (like PaaS, IaaS).

Baby care can be provided by nanny at family control environment (like Private Cloud), can be provided for different communities like office employees, religions (similar to Community Cloud), Baby Care common facilities (like Public Cloud), or within a public baby care have private centers as well (like Hybrid Cloud).

Software defined environments

Software defined environments can be composed of software-defined data center (SDDC), software-defined network (SDN), software-defined compute (SDC), software-defined storage (SDS), and software-defined infrastructure (SDI), and refer to vision for IT resources to extend virtualization such as abstraction, pooling, and automation to all of the data center's resources and services to achieve IT as a service (SDDC); an approach to networking that allows management of network services through abstraction of lower level functionality (SDN); software that manages the storage infrastructure (SDS); and collective of compute, storage and network and the intelligence for managing the infrastructure (SDI). Software-defined environment (SDE) enables capturing information about workloads and how information is processed, enabling management of the SLAs. OpenStack is a framework that brings together vendors to build a consistent view and see how their products plug into the API-driven behavioral model of an environment.

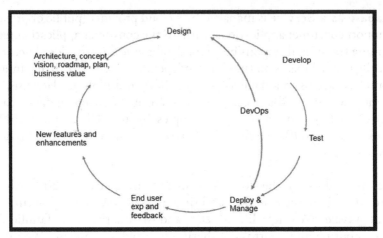

Fig 2.1.9 The Organic Cloud Evolution Ecosystem

Governance in the context of cloud computing

Cloud computing enables ubiquitous, convenient, on-demand network access to a shared pool of configurable computing resources that can be quickly provisioned and released with minimal effort. Cloud architectures leverage Internet-accessible on-demand services. Applications built on cloud architectures use the underlying computing infrastructure only when it is needed, and then quickly release the resources after the job is done. In operation, application scales elastically based on resource needs.

As is with all else, the importance of Governance is utmost while embracing cloud. Companies need to analyze their existing processes to determine the areas where what can be automated in an efficient way when offered as a cloud service, and what are the candidate applications that can leverage these and other provider's cloud services. The segregation of resources and the target applications these would serve, and then matching resources to targets, including shared resources, would be the first step towards cloud initiation. This would tell us as to what we would need and why, and then plan on how to provision it in an adequate manner. Such matching can be the very part of a governance process, so that capacities are properly planned and met.

Approvals and exception processes need to be documented and agreed upon by all key stakeholders to become effective. Typically, existing processes can contain several manual steps that may slow down the overall provisioning process. In a cloud environment where IT services are rapidly deployed, such steps can be automated. The governance process can address all Security related concerns, and ensure compliance to mandated corporate standards.

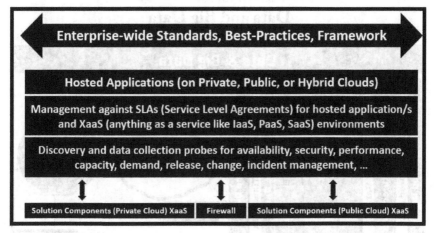

Fig 2.1.10 A simple cloud computing Governance Model
(alerts generated from probes are tapped for next best action)

Sub Section 2.2

Data and Big Data

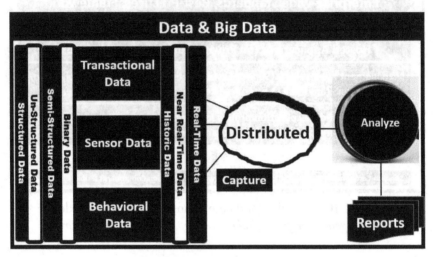

Fig 2.2 Data and Big Data

Chapter 2.2.1. Data Management

What is Data, what's the purpose of data management, and how to accomplish its outcome?

Data is same as 'value' i.e. what's the value of a particular item i.e. what's my height, what's my salary, what's the capital of 'USA' and so on.

To use the data, values of various things may need to be joined to convert **data** into **information** for optimal use. As an example, to find some information about the family, data for all related family members may need to be joined and then combined. Data may need to be joined even for taking an action – like to place an order, we may need to know data about the customer, products, and more as needed.

In short, **Data** is the input and **Information** is the outcome of **Data Management**. Here are various examples of similar input and outcomes:

- Just like, this Book is the input and using it for desired result is the outcome

- Resources are the input and converting resources into services using capabilities is part of Service Management
- Using people resources and utilizing their skills to have best win-win situation for employees and employers is part of People Management
- Looking at various qualities and minimizing the quality variations (sigma), and providing best quality with proper prediction is part of Quality Management
- Looking at all wastage, and minimizing wastage is part of Wastage Management (MUDA)
- Using various resources and optimizing their usage to provide best delivery is part of Project Management
- Same goes for others areas like Financial Management, Politics Management, Investment Management, Family Management, Social Management and so on…

For any use of data, first of all, some relationship needs to be maintained between various parts of data before they can be joined. Many years back, it started with **Hierarchical** model, then **Network** model, followed by **Relational** model.

Chapter 2.2.2. Hierarchical Model:

Data is organized as a tree structure with a hierarchy of a parent and its children data segments. A record can have repeating information, generally in the child data segments. Data is maintained in a series of records, with a set of field values attached to it. It collects values of a specific record together as a record type. To create linkage between record types, a hierarchical model uses Parent-Child Relationships.

In a hierarchical data model, there's no many-many relationship between record type but only 1 to many.

As an example, if there's a company with many employees – the company has its record and each employee has its record and the relationship shows all employees related to the company i.e. a company record will be related to multiple employee records. But an employee is related to just one employer. What happens if an employee works for more than one company?

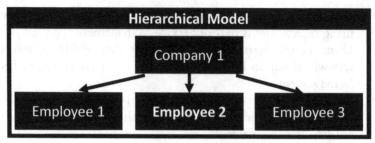

Fig 2.2.1 Hierarchical Model

Chapter 2.2.3. Network Model:

Main purpose of Network Model was to allow many-to-many relationships in data. In 1971, the Conference on Data Systems Languages (CODASYL) formally defined the network model. The basic data modeling construct in the network model is the set construct. A set consists of an owner record type, a set name, and a member record type. A member record type can have that role in more than one set, hence the multiparent concept was supported. An owner record type can also be a member or owner in another set. The data model is a simple network, and link and intersection record types (called junction records) may exist, as well as sets between them. Thus, the complete network of relationships is represented by several pairwise sets; in each set, some (or one) record type is owner (at the tail of the network arrow) and one or more record types are members (at the head of the relationship arrow). Usually, a set defines a 1:M relationship, although 1:1 is permitted. The CODASYL network model is based on mathematical set theory.

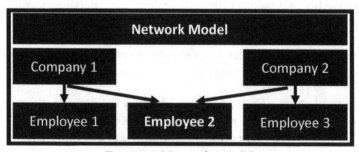

Fig 2.2.2 Network Model

Chapter 2.2.4. Relational Model

RDBMS (Relational Database Management System) is a database created on the relational model developed by E.F. Codd. A relational database allows the definition of data structures, storage, retrieval operations, and integrity constraints. In such a database, the data and relationship between them are organized in tables. A table is a collection of records and each record in a table contains the same fields. A record is called as 'Tuple', the order in which the tuples are captured or the order in which various fields are captured doesn't matter.

Any fields for tables can be related and which fields to display from which records, what conditions, what order etc. is all decided by operations performed on Relational tables (called Structured Query Language or SQL) that will be explained later. The Relational database model is based on the Relational Algebra.

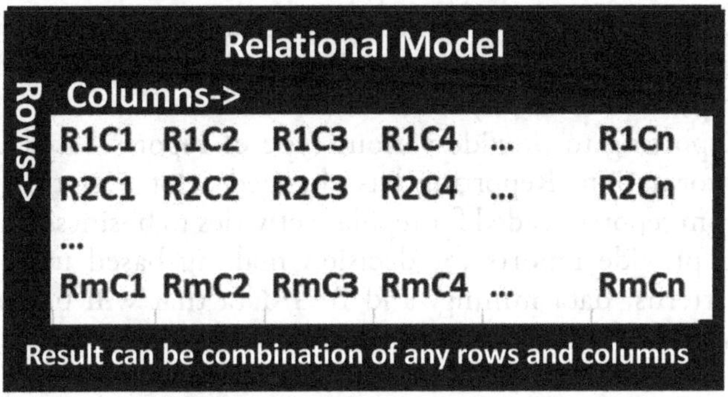

Fig 2.2.3 Relational Model

Here's an example that shows some properties of an RDBMS table - Let's say we want to capture data about various states that includes fields:

- Name of the State
- Name of the Country, state belongs
- It's Capital
- It's Population
- Date Population was computed
- Number of Cities
- Chief of State's Name
- ....

In what order, we add records doesn't matter (although typically all systems keep track of when a record (tuple) was added and their unique ID number

Some fields may be added later and in what order they are captured doesn't matter as long as each value is assigned to field name.

Each field may have special properties and the value assigned to that field may need to follow those restrictions (based upon the RDBMS tool) like:

- If the field is numeric, its value must be numeric and this value may depend upon the size of the numeric field (like byte, integer, long integer....)
- Value may be restricted to include only 'a set of values' (like 'M' or 'F' for gender)

Main purpose of Data Management is to convert data into information for two main reasons i.e.-

1. Use the data for processing of various transactions like Airline Reservation based upon real-time status of what's available, ERP for enterprise resource planning, and almost all activities that impact the inventory
2. Reporting to provide various type of reports based upon the information. Reporting has changed a lot over time starting from reports needed for regular activities to business intelligence to provide reports for decision making based upon historic patterns, data mining, and BIG data that will be covered in later chapters

Data Repository that is used to provide processing of various transactions plus all transactional reporting is called *Transactional Database.*

Major Properties of RDBMS

- **RDBMS Data**
- **Data Normalization**
- **Data Modeling**

RDBMS Data

RDBMS Data includes details for all entities and their relationships, such as tables, all attributes (fields) within the table and their relationships

As an example, let's say we define 3 tables i.e. Customer_Table, Product_Table, and Orders_Table with fields shown below:

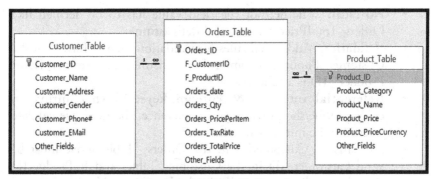

Fig 2.2.4 RDBMS Sample

Define Fields (Schema)

We may need to define some details of each field such as:

- Orders Qty must be Numeric without any decimal value
- Orders_PricePerItem, Orders_TaxRate, Orders_TotalPrice, and Product_Price must be numeric with decimal value
- Orders_Date must be a valid date, rest of the fields can be text
- We may also define maximum size for each text field, and type of numeric field (such as small or large like Byte, Integer, Long Integer…)
- Moreover, we might define that the only allowed values for a particular value category are 'High', 'Medium', or 'Low'
- Zero to many (0-infinity (∞)) relationship between Customer_Table and Orders_Table as well as between Product_Table and Orders_Table i.e. there can be multiple orders for each customer (or unrelated), and multiple orders for each product (or unrelated)
- There can be more details such as value range, whether/not the value must be provided
- Defines additional constraints as part of data definition to enhance the quality of data captured, ease of joining data, and provide a good response to provide desired information such as
- **Primary Key:** Customer_ID is the primary key for Customer_Table, Product _ID is the primary key for Products Table, and F_CustomerID plus F_Product ID together are the primary key for the Orders _Table. Primary Key means there can be only one record with the same value for all fields of the Primary Key and it must have a value

- **No Null:** Whether/not the field value has to be defined like Orders_TotalPrice can't be null (let's assume)
- **Validation:** Additional rules for validation such as format of the Customer_Phone#, or some rules to ensure the Customer_ID or Product _ID is a valid ID
- **Referential integrity & Foreign keys:** If while hiring an employee, he/she provides you a reference, shouldn't we validate to ensure the integrity of reference?
- Similarly, F_CustomerID in the Orders _Table above must be valid Customer_ID in the Customer_Table, and F_ProductID must be a valid Product_ID in the Product_Table, if referential integrity is provided.
- These are defined as Foreign keys i.e. F_CustomerID in Orders_Table may be a foreign key related to Customer_ID field in Customer_Table, and F_ProductID in Orders_Table may be a foreign key related to Product_ID field in Product_Table. If they have the referential integrity that means any F_CustomerID in Orders_Table must be present as Customer_ID in Customer_Table, and F_ProductID must be present as Product_ID in the Product_Table

  The term used to define RDBMS details, such as those described above, is called Schema.

SQL: The major way to view the results of data in RDBMS is by using SQL (Structured Query Language). According to ANSI (American National Standards Institute), it is the standard language for relational database management systems.

SQL allows to select any number of fields to retrieve from multiple data sources (tables), lets you define how to co-relate those tables, lets you define any conditions to decide how to filter the data and retrieve, allows to sort the results in the order you like, allows you to aggregate any portion of the data as well (totals or sub-totals).

Here's a simple SQL example to get details for customer_ID = 1 and related to USD (US Dollar) ordered by Order Data with the latest dates first:

SELECT

    Customer_Name, Customer_Address, Customer_Phone#,
    Customer_EMail,
    Product_Category, Product_Name, Product_Price
    Currency,

> Orders_ID, Orders_Date, Orders_Qty, Orders_Price
> PerItem, Orders_Qty*Orders_PricePerItem AS NetPrice,
> Orders_TaxRate, Orders_TaxRate*NetPrice AS
> TotalTax, Orders_TotalPrice
>
> FROM Customer_Table, Product_Table, Orders_Table
>
> WHERE Customer_ID = F_CustomerID AND Product_ID
> = F_ProductID
>   AND Customer_ID =1 AND Product_PriceCurrency
>   = "USD"
>
> ORDER BY Orders_date DESC

Chapter 2.2.5. Data Normalization and Modeling

One of the important characteristics for transaction processing is called Normalization i.e. how to structure data properly. Main purpose for Normalization is

- Easy to Add new data
- Easy to Update Existing Data
- Easy to Delete Existing Data

As an example, let's say we want to capture data for various patients and the procedure performed on them by doctors in a hospital i.e. here's the captured data structured

	Doctor ID	Doctor Name	Patient ID	Patient Name	Date of Procedure	Medication	Side Effects
1	1	Doc1					
2			1	Patient1			
3	1	Doc1	1	Patient1	1/1/2016	Medicine1	Rash
4	2	Doc2	2	Patient2	2/1/2016	Medicine1	Rash
5	2	Doc2	1	Patient1	4/1/2016	Medicine2	Rash
6	1	Doc3	2	Patient3	5/1/2016	Medicine2	Headache
7	1	Doc1					

Fig 2.2.5 Unnormalized Data

- First record contains fields for a new doctor
- Second record contains fields for a new patient
- Third record contains procedure details for doctor/patient whose records already exist

- Fourth record contains details procedure details for doctor/patient whose records are also added only when they are involved in this procedure
- Records fifth and sixth are more procedures. Record 6th also includes situation where the name of the doctor and patient changed
- Record 7th is same record added for an existing doctor
- …...

Problems: First of all, same record can be repeated and therefore, there's no way to find a particular record based upon certain set of values. Moreover, there are duplicate names for Doctor ID 1 and Patient ID 2.

First Normal Form of Normalization requires each record (tuple) must have a **Primary Key** i.e. set of fields that can't be repeated. Let's assume that Doctor_ID, Patient_ID, and Date_of_Procedure is the primary key (Primary Key fields are shown as underlined) i.e. same doctor can have just once procedure on a specific patient on a specific date.

So here comes the First Normal Form example of same data

	Doctor ID	Patient ID	Date of Procedure	Doctor Name	Patient Name	Medication	Side Effects
1	1	1	1/1/2016	Doc1	Patient1	Medicine1	Rash
2	1	2	5/1/2016	Doc1	Patient3	Medicine2	Headache
3	2	1	4/1/2016	Doc3	Patient1	Medicine2	Rash
4	2	2	2/1/2016	Doc2	Patient2	Medicine1	Rash

Fig 2.2.6 First Normal Form-Primary Key

Attributes related to primary key are called Key Attributes (Doctor_ID, Patient_ID, and Date_of_Procedure) and other attributes are called Non-Key Attributes.

Problems: If a new doctor comes up, or a new patient comes up without any procedures yet, those records can't be added. Moreover, if we want to update the doctor ID 1's name from Doc1 to Doc3 and the process aborts in the middle, half the records may be updated and not the other half. In other words, data update is also a problem.

Therefore, Second Normal Form requires **Full Functional Dependency** i.e. all non-key attributes should be dependent on all key-attributes and not a sub-set of them. Like in this example Doctor_Name depends only on Doctor_ID and similarly Patient_Name depends only on Patient_ID.

Doctor's Table		Patient's Table	
Doctor ID	Doctor Name	Patient ID	Patient Name
1	1	Doc1	1	1	Patient1
2	2	Doc2	2	2	Patient2

	Procedure's Table				
	Doctor ID	Patient ID	Date of Procedure	Medication	Side Effects
1	1	1	1/1/2016	Medicine1	Rash
2	1	2	5/1/2016	Medicine2	Headache
3	2	1	4/1/2016	Medicine2	Rash
4	2	2	2/1/2016	Medicine1	Rash

Fig 2.2.7 Second Normal Form
(Full Functional Dependency)

So, we divide one table into three separate tables as per second normal form shown above. Easy to add/delete/update a record for doctor, patient, procedure and record for patient/doctor may not be deleted until there's no procedure for them if there's referential integrity condition.

Problems: If we want to find out the side effects of a particular medicine, there can be all sort of problems since there can be any kind of wrong entry for medicine, besides multiple side effects.

Therefore, Third Normal Form requires **No Transitional Dependency** i.e. no non-key attribute should be dependent on another non-key attribute. In this case, assuming side effect depends on Medication.

So, finally we divide this into four separate tables per third normal form i.e.

Doctor's Table		Patient's Table	
Doctor ID	Doctor Name	Patient ID	Patient Name
1	1	Doc1	1	1	Patient1
2	2	Doc2	2	2	Patient2

Side Effect's Table	
Medication	Side Effects
1	Medicine1	Rash
2	Medicine2	Rash
3	Medicine2	Headache

	Procedure's Table			
	Doctor ID	Patient ID	Date of Procedure	Medication
1	1	1	1/1/2016	Medicine1
2	1	2	5/1/2016	Medicine2
3	2	1	4/1/2016	Medicine2
4	2	2	2/1/2016	Medicine1

Fig 2.2.8 Third Normal Form
(Full Functional Dependency, No Transitional Dependency)

E-R Diagram: (Entity-Relationship Diagram)

Data modeling for RDBMS covers basics and architecture to define the data. One of the basics is called as the **E-R Diagram.**

An E-R Diagram for data defines relationship between main entities (like tables and fields)

Here's an example of an E-R Diagram as covered under **'Data Normalization'** above showing a doctor or a patient can have multiple (0 to infinite) procedures. Similarly, a medicine can be provided to multiple side-effects (0 to infinite) across procedures.

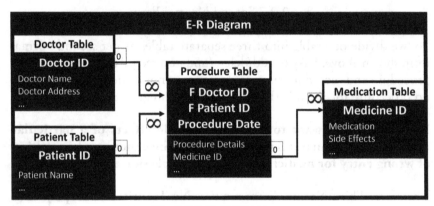

Fig 2.2.9 E-R Diagram

Data Modeling: At a high level, the data modeling is defined in 3 steps i.e. Conceptual Data Model, Logical Data Model, and Physical Data Model.

Conceptual Data Model

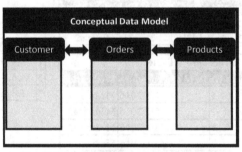

Fig 2.2.10 Conceptual Data Model

- Includes the important entities (like tables) and the relationships between them
- No attribute (like fields) is specified
- No primary key is specified
- At this level, the data modeler attempts to identify the highest-level relationships among the different entities

Logical Data Model

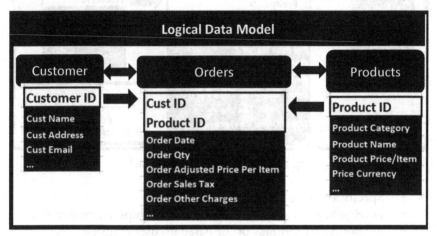

Fig 2.2.11 Logical Data Model

- Includes all entities and relationships among them
- All attributes for each entity are specified
- The primary key for each entity is specified
- Foreign keys (keys identifying the relationship between different entities) are specified
- Normalization occurs at this level
- At this level, the data modeler attempts to describe the data in as much detail as possible, without practicality to how they will be physically implemented in the database

Main steps for designing the logical data model are as follows:

- Identify all entities
- Specify primary keys for all entities
- Find the relationships between different entities
- Find all attributes for each entity
- Resolve many-to-many relationships
- Normalization

Physical Data Model

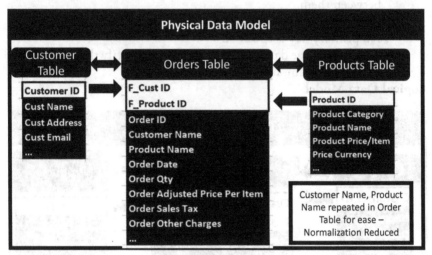

Fig 2.2.12 Physical Data Model

- Specification for all tables and columns
- Foreign keys are used to identify relationships between tables
- De-normalization may occur based on user requirements
- Physical considerations may cause the physical data model to be quite different from the logical data model
- At this level, the data modeler will specify how the logical data model will be realized in the database schema

The steps for physical data model design are as follows:

1. Convert entities into tables
2. Convert relationships into foreign keys
3. Convert attributes into columns
4. Modify the physical data model based on physical and practical constraints/requirements

Chapter 2.2.6. Transactional Database

Normal RDBMS database that provide processing and reporting for all transactions is a **Transactional Database** i.e. it serves as the data repository for all transactions.

Processing for a Transactional database is termed as **OLTP** (On-line Transaction Processing), which is typically characterized by a good number of on-line transactions (INSERT, UPDATE, DELETE). The main purpose of OLTP is to keep very fast query processing, maintaining data integrity in multi-access environments and effective measurement by number of transactions per second.

Since transactions include maintaining data in real-time, all transaction processing can be done based on the most recent transaction status (like when one wants to reserve an airline ticket, the status must be updated before the next person should try to check the status or make a reservation). It normally requires a transactional database close to third normal form.

It takes a good amount of time to read/update the disk I/O and if there are a large number of transactions going on by multiple users, it will take time to read the desired result from disk for user1, then if user1 makes an update, those changes should be updated to disk before user2 wants to read the data. So, all updates must be completed before next user can read them.

A method to perform faster data read/update is to minimize disk I/O's and keep data in memory (called **Caching**). Based upon various patterns and the amount of memory available, most frequently data is kept in cache. When a user wants to read a data, it's first checked if available in cache, otherwise disk I/O is used.

If a user updates a data, that update is also performed in the cache and periodically updated to disk. What happens if the data server aborts working due to any reason – the update in cache is not written to disk I/O and thus all updates to cache are lost. One way to track all updates is keeping track of (log) all updates on disk since updated to disk last time. If the system stops working due to any reason, once the system restarts – it checks any pending logs and those transactions are processed to update the disk (recovery process) before the access is provided to users. That provides a much better performance and a recovery process if needed.

Also, since a transactional database is the real original data, there have to be proper tools to provide backups, fault tolerance mechanisms, and recovery process in case the data needs to be restored. To allow quick data retrieval, it's common to maintain master data and its read-only copies at multiple sources.

Most of the applications may have their own transactional data, although some applications may share some transactional data. In other words, there can be a large number of transactional data repositories within a business and many of them may be using completely different technologies and tools (combination of excel spreadsheet, MS Access, Oracle, SQL Server, Word Documents, or even just paper documents…).

When a business upgrades their application (aka Apps Modernization), they also need to migrate their old data to the new transactional database. Typically, the applications are upgraded after very long time and the technology would have changed substantially by then. The technology involved with the old data may be quite different than the technology associated with the new data. The old data is, sometimes, called as *Legacy Data.*

How to migrate the data from previous sources to the new target transactional data will be covered under Chapter 2.2.8 'ETL (Extraction, Transformation, & Loading) Process' along with migration of data from transactional data to data warehouse

Chapter 2.2.7. Data Warehouse

Transactional data may be maintained across multiple data repositories using different tools that may be completely diversified.

The leaders of a business may need to analyze the historic patterns, trends, and may act based upon what happened in the past. As an example, the transaction data for HR, Infrastructure, various applications, and many other business units may be completely isolated and to understand the historic pattern, the data across them may need to be related before any decision can be made. To co-relate the data, it can take very long-time and since data across different sources may be referenced at different time, it may not be completely synchronous.

If we need to do many data synchronizations across various transaction data, that will add additional overhead on the transactional data processing speed and may impact the speed of transaction processing. The purpose of data analysis/analytics is to get the consolidated view of all related transaction data mainly just for reading and not for updating. The terms Analysis and Analytics are similar but Analysis was used for DW to analyze the data whereas Analytics is used to analyze the data in Big Data. Analysis is more concerned with analyzing the historic data for various patterns whereas Analytics is concerned with more complex recommendations.

In other words, all data is maintained in individual transactional databases, but that data needs to be consolidated on a periodic basis with least impact on transaction processing while retrieving the consolidated data. That is the main purpose of Data Warehouse.

In short, a data warehouse needs to retrieve desired information from various transactional data repositories, find ways to co-relate them as needed based upon decision making requirements, consolidate and summarize periodically (when the transaction processing impact is minimized), and build a new consolidated data repository that can be used for data analysis. Since this is a completely different data, its analysis has no impact on transaction data processing (OLTP). The process of data analysis is called **OLAP** (On-Line Analytic Processing) as opposed to OLTP (On-Line Transaction Processing) related to Transaction Database.

Data Warehouse is mainly read-only and its purpose is to provide very fast results. So, most of the data warehouses are not Third Normal Form but Second Normal Form. Moreover, since this is not the original data, normally there's no backup requirement.

How to migrate the transactional data periodically to populate the data ware house, will also be covered under Chapter 2.2.8 'ETL (Extraction, Transformation, & Loading) Process' along with migration of data from legacy data to transactional data.

Here are some high-level details of Data Warehouse:

Table Types:

Typically, a Data Warehouse uses a dimensional data structure where it includes 2 types of tables i.e. one that contains the attributes that can be summarized (Fact Table) based upon the level of details needed and the other table contains the attributes that defines how to scan and summarize Fact Data (Dimensional Table).

Fact Tables:

In data warehousing, a fact table consists of the measurements, metrics or facts of a business process. It is often located at the center of a data warehouse, surrounded by dimension tables.

Fact tables, typically provide the additive values which act as independent variables by which dimensional attributes are analyzed - often defined by the term **grain.**

The grain of a fact table represents the most atomic (lowest) level by which the facts are captured. As an example, if we keep lowest level of the sales fact table as "Sales volume by Day by Product by Store". Each record in this fact table is therefore uniquely defined by a day, product and store which defines its grain. We can summarize that to any higher level (i.e. Sales for a set of products, by a set of stores, for multiple days) but can't get the lower level value using data warehouse i.e. we can't get the sales by hours, since at the lowest level (grain), data is captured in the Fact Table by day.

If the need for data warehouse (decision making) is such that we don't need to know any level lower than the grain, there's no need to capture the lower level data and thus spend more time and storage. Changes can be made later on, if needed.

Fact Table Types

1. **Transaction Grain Fact Table**: A transaction grain fact table is based upon the measurements taken at a given location and given time. Example could be the sales, time etc. It can contain zero or an extremely large number of values. They have very low-level grain i.e. each instance at each location and time.

2. **Periodic Snapshot Fact Table**: Periodic Snapshot Fact Tables define values over specific periods (like totals for each month). Although the count is defined but it can start from zero and gets added as time passes. Grain level is pretty high.

3. **Accumulating Snapshot Fact Table**: Provides accumulated values between defined beginning and ending dimensions like values between 'Order Date' and 'Invoice Date'. The grain is nether too low, nor too high.

4. **Fact-less Fact Table**: There's no Fact Data for Fact-less fact tables. An example could be an accident by an individual, a vehicle, and location. Although there could be dimensions and whether/not an incident occurred, but no fact data count or amount value.

Dimensional Tables:

Dimensional table provides various set of attributes (dimensions) that are directly related to the Fact Table and those set of attributes can be used to define the conditions related to those attributes and how to summarize the values from the Fact Tables to provide the result.

As the example shown above in the Fact Tables, where we are keeping the Fact tables using Sales volume by Day by Product by Store, here's one example of 3 dimension tables and the Fact Table:

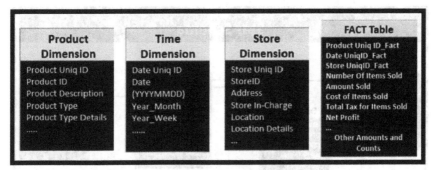

Fig 2.2.13 Dimension and Fact Tables

The Fact and the dimension tables are co-related by the 3 keys and thus any question such as:

Compare the 'Net Profit' for all Stores in a specific location for certain 'Product Types' during certain special days (viz. Black Friday...).

That can be easily summarized.

Data Warehouse Schemas

There are 3 main type of structures (Schemas) defined for the Data Warehouse called **Star Schema**, **Snowflake Schema**, and **Fact Constellation Schema.**

Star Schema

Contains a Fact Table with direct relationship with all dimensions and it is typically in Second Normal Form.

In the example below, the Product Type Details are dependent only on Product Type (Transitional Dependence) and same is true for Location and Location Details and thus there is transactional dependence and therefore, these are not exactly in third normal form but second normal form.

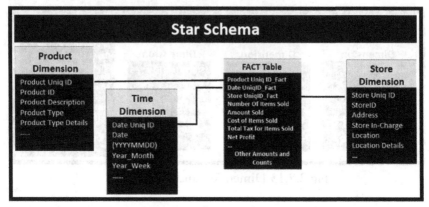

Fig 2.2.14 Star Schema

Snowflake Schema

The dimension table can be further detailed to change 2nd normal form towards 3rd normal form i.e. the Product Dimension can be split into 2 dimensions (Product and Product Type and avoiding transactional dependence) and same with Store Dimension as shown below:

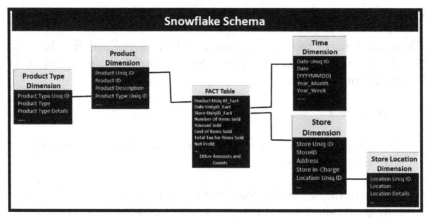

Fig 2.2.15 Snowflake Schema

Fact Constellation Schema

There can be more than one Fact Tables shown below, where even the dimensions can be split into 3rd normal form.

The example below shows, besides facts by product, day, and store; we can have another fact table that provides facts by customer besides product, day, and store.

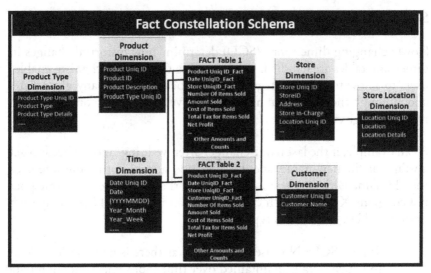

Fig 2.2.16 Fact Constellation Schema

Lookup Table:

Lookup table provides detailed information about the attributes. For example, the lookup table for Quarter attribute would include a list of all of the quarters available in the data warehouse. Each row (each quarter) may have several fields, one for the unique ID that identifies the quarter, and one or more additional fields that specify how that particular quarter is represented on a report (for example, first quarter of 2001 may be represented as "Q1 2001" or "2001 Q1").

Surrogate Keys:

Surrogate keys are primary/foreign key values (not the keys) that co-relate various tables (like the dimension tables and fact tables) but have no relationship to the unique record they identify. Various Unique ID's shown in the diagrams above are examples of Surrogate Keys. Most often, surrogate keys are deployed as sequential integer values and are unique.

Main advantage of surrogate keys is high performance since these keys can be pretty small, flexible, and internally maintained.

As an example, if the customer ID is a 9-digit number, and their values are 123736443, 893673434, and 543746434; their surrogate values could just be 1, 2, and 3.

Slowly Changing Dimensions:

Slowly changing dimensions (SCD) determine how historical changes in dimension tables are handled. Implementing the SCD mechanism enables users to know to which category an item belongs to, on any given date, and although the dimension has changed over time, which one we should refer to at a given time.

As an example, if the last name changes after wedding, and we need to get a value for the new name, should it include sum of both names, replace the old name with the new name, or keep them separate etc. Same goes if a company X merges with company Y - and there could be many such examples. Here are various types of SCDs.

- Type 0 SCD: Not used frequently, as there is no specific logic as to which data is maintained over time. So, some dimension data may be overwritten and other may stay unchanged over the time and it can result in confusion
- Type 1 SCD - No history is kept in the database. The new, changed data simply overwrites old entries. Main use of this approach is to overwrite data (over time) caused by correcting data quality errors (misspells, data consolidations, trimming spaces, language specific characters etc.). Type 1 SCD is easy to maintain and used mainly when losing the ability to track the old history is not an issue
- In the Type 2 SCD model the whole history is stored in the database. An additional dimension record is created and the segmenting between the old record values and the new (current) value is easy to extract and the history is clear. The fields 'effective date' and 'current indicator' are very often used in that dimension
- Type 3 SCD - Only the information about a previous value of a dimension is written into the database. An 'old 'or 'previous' column is created which stores the immediate and previous attribute. In Type 3 SCD users are able to describe history immediately and can report both forward and backward from the change.
- However, this model can't track all historical changes, when a dimension changes more than once. It would require creating next columns to store historical data and could make the whole data warehouse schema very complex

- Type 4 SCD idea is to store all historical changes in a separate historical data table for each of the dimensions.

ODS (Operational Data Store):

An operational data store (or "ODS") is a database designed to integrate data from multiple sources to facilitate operations, analysis and reporting. Because the data originates from multiple sources, the integration often may involve various types of checks/transformation like validation, cleansing, de-duplication, data conforming, business rule enforcement and others. An ODS is usually designed to contain low level or atomic (indivisible) data such as transactions and prices as opposed to aggregated or summarized data such as net contributions. Aggregated data is usually stored in the Data Warehouse but is kept at the lowest grain level in ODS and the data can be used even for transactional reporting.

Data Mart:

A data mart (DM) is a specialized domain of a data warehouse (DW), typically a subset of the data warehouse targeted to a specific line of business, product suite, or customer segment. Like data warehouse, data marts contain a snapshot of operational data that helps business people to strategize based on analyses of past trends and experiences, with a very specific focus.

The key difference between data warehouse and data mart is the creation of a data mart predicated on a specific, predefined need for a certain grouping and configuration of select data. A data mart configuration emphasizes easy access to relevant information.

EDW (Enterprise Data Warehouse):

An enterprise data warehouse is the data warehouse across multiple business units within an enterprise. Although the exact difference between a Data Mart, Data Warehouse, and Enterprise Data Warehouse may vary, the main purpose is that Data Warehouse is a subset of Enterprise Data Warehouse, and Data Mart is a subset of Data Warehouse.

OLAP (On Line Analytic Processing):

For people on the business side, the key feature out of the above list is "Multidimensional." In other words, the ability to analyze metrics in different dimensions such as time, geography, gender, product, etc. For example, if sales for a company goes up, what region is most responsible for this increase? Which store in this region is most responsible for the increase? What particular product category or categories contributed the most to the increase? Answering these types of questions in order means that you are performing an OLAP analysis.

OLTP is used for transaction purpose whereas OLAP is used for Analytic purpose.

There are 3 ways to implement the outcome of OLAP i.e. Multidimensional, Relational, or Hybrid OLAP.

Analytic MOLAP (Multidimensional On-Line Processing):

This is the more traditional way of OLAP analysis. In MOLAP, data is stored in a multidimensional cube. The storage is not in the relational database, but in proprietary formats. The data is already built and stored based upon pre-defined multi-dimensions.

Advantages:

- Excellent performance: MOLAP cubes are built for fast data retrieval, and is optimal for slicing and dicing operations
- Can perform complex calculations: All calculations have been pre-generated when the cube is created. Hence, complex calculations are not only doable, but they can be retrieved at a fast speed

Disadvantages:

- Limited in the amount of data it can handle: Because all calculations are performed and stored when the cube is built, it is difficult to include a large amount of data in the cube itself. This is not to say that the data in the cube cannot be derived from a large amount of data. Indeed, this is possible. But in this case, only summary-level information will be included in the cube itself
- Requires additional investment: Cube technologies are often proprietary and do not already exist in the organization. Therefore, to adopt MOLAP technology, normally additional investments in human and capital resources is needed

ROLAP (Relational On-Line Processing):

ROLAP typically provides additional processing to data that is maintained in RDBMS. This methodology relies on manipulating the data stored in the relational database (RDBMS) to give the appearance of traditional OLAP's slicing and dicing functionality. In essence, each action of slicing and dicing is equivalent to adding a "WHERE" clause in the SQL statement.

Advantages:

- Can handle large amounts of data: The data size limitation of ROLAP technology is the limitation on data size of the underlying relational database. In other words, ROLAP itself places no limitation on data amount
- Can leverage functionalities inherent in the relational database: Often, relational database already comes with a host of functionalities. ROLAP technologies, since they sit on top of the relational database, can therefore leverage these functionalities
- Save money since typical ROLAP tools are quite expensive

Disadvantages:

- Performance can be slow: Because each ROLAP report is essentially an SQL query (or multiple SQL queries) in the relational database, the query time can be long if the underlying data size is large
- Limited by SQL functionalities: Because ROLAP technology mainly relies on generating SQL statements to query the relational database, and SQL statements do not fit all needs (for example, it is difficult to perform complex calculations using SQL), ROLAP technologies are therefore traditionally limited by what SQL can do. ROLAP vendors have mitigated this risk by building into the tool out-of-the-box complex functions as well as the ability to allow users to define their own functions

HOLAP (Hybrid On-Line Processing):

HOLAP technologies attempt to combine the advantages of MOLAP and ROLAP. For summary-type information, HOLAP leverages cube technology for faster performance. When detail information is needed, HOLAP can "drill through" from the cube into the underlying relational data.

Chapter 2.2.8. ETL (Extraction, Transformation, and Loading) Process

When we need to get the data from multiple sources and consolidate the data to a target base, it's called data migration. We need to follow some good process for data migration to provide good quality. ETL is the most common process to migrate data from multiple sources where Source of Data refers to incoming data (that contain various diverse types of data) to Target data (aka destination data).

Target data schema (format/structure) is decided based upon the data needed for various types of output processing and reporting.

Data migration is typically involved during 2 major activities:

1. When we upgrade an application, or initiate a new application (aka Application Modernization), that requires migration of data from previous data sources to the new transactional database. Sometimes the old data sources are called Legacy Data. Moreover, it can be a

onetime process i.e. once all the old data gets migrated and the old application gets discarded, there's no need to migrate data from the old data sources – although in case the migration involved multiple phases and old application and the new application are being used simultaneously, the data between the two may need to be synchronized (aka data bridging) until the old application gets discarded. More details for data bridging are provided later in this chapter under Data Sync-up (Data Bridging) – Only for Legacy Data Migration.

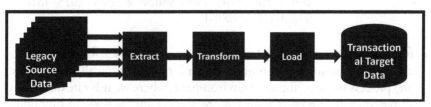

Fig 2.2.17 Legacy Data Migration

2. For data warehousing where we need to migrate data from transactional data that may reside across multiple transactional data sources.

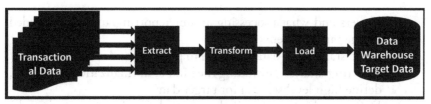

Fig 2.2.18 Transactional Data to Data Warehouse Migration

Major differences between data migration from Legacy Data to Transactional Data and Transactional Data to Data Warehouse include:

- Where the need to migrate legacy data to transactional data is a onetime requirement, the purpose of data warehouse is to get a consolidated view of transactional data on a regular basis and thus we need to periodically migrate the transactional data to DW
- The need for DW may include building of Data Marts. Either, we can first build Data Marts and then consolidate to DW or EDW; or we can start with DW or EDW and then decompose them into Data Marts. These 2

methodologies are called Bottom-Up or Top-Down approaches and Data Warehousing expert Bill Inmon (1) initiated the Bottom-Up approach whereas Ralph Kimball (2) initiated the Top-Down approach.

(1) Building the Data Warehouse, W. H. Inmon, Wiley Publishing, Inc. 2005, ISBN# 978-0-7645-9944-6

(2) The Data Warehouse Toolkit: The Definitive Guide to Dimensional Modeling, Ralph Kimball and Margy Ross, John Wiley & Sons, 2013, ISBN# 978-1-118-53080-1

Before going live with the Data migration of real data for a particular phase in a production environment, data migration is typically an iterative (agile) process in a development environment, where we migrate data from multiple sources. We keep adding more sources and/or keep adding more migration logic and keep repeating the data migration process. These are normally called Mock Runs.

Here are the high-level steps needed for data migration before we start going over ETL process details:

1. Understand what processing and/or reporting/analysis is needed on the target system
2. Understand what data is needed to provide the desired processing/reporting/analysis, including the kind of normalization needed i.e. define high level schema for target data
3. Define multiple phases if the entire data migration needs to be completed in more than 1 phase
4. For each phase, find where are the sources of data and if needed adjust the target schema
5. Build various environments like – development environment where various iterations of data migration can be developed, test environment where data migration can be tested, production environment where real data can be migrated
6. Besides data migration, various requirements are also used to define the required infrastructure, and other resources

It's common to use Staging Areas where data is temporarily stored during various ETL stages. Staging provides 3 main purposes including:

- Auditing: Maintain record of all operations performed on data. This should include enough details to serve the purpose of

  1. Trend analysis on data conversions and time taken
  2. Failed attempts including security violations
  3. Input for capacity planning and performance planning

- Backup: Can server as a backup repository during particular stage
- Recovery: In case of any problem during a process, data can be retrieved to the staging area and process can re-start from there

Here are some details for the ETL process.

Data Extraction (E)

Data extraction requires strong collaboration with various SMEs (Subject Matter Experts) for the existing data sources/applications to provide information for the following areas:

- All data sources
- Field specs for each table including any special and outdated situations such as Packed Decimal types, Julian Date types, and so on
- Primary Keys, Relationship between sources via Foreign Keys and E-R diagrams
- Constraints, and counts
- Performance Issues
- Order of processing and dependence across data sources
- Any Known Issues

Data Extraction will also decide high level method to extract data from each source.

At a high level, it's useful to define at least 3 source data details i.e.

1. Source Data Summary:
   It provides information about each of the source data such as - type of source data, primary key, description, any comments, approximate total record count, what data is useful for target, approximate records selected, how to get the data etc...

   Moreover, it's useful to get additional details i.e.

- Push/Pull: Whether to push the data from source to target or target can pull from the source
- Dump/Link: Whether the data has to be dumped and then collected, or it can be directly linked. Typically, data can be linked based upon compatibility between tools.
- Data/Document: Whether the source data is a document or data
- Electronic/Paper: There could be situations where some of the source data is only in paper and that has to be scanned to document or converted to data

Shown below is a data template that provides summary of all source data where Source ID is the unique ID for each source.

							Source Data Summary								
Source ID	Name	Source Type	Description	~Record Count	Primary Key	~Record Size (Bytes)	Comments	Filtering Logic		~Target Record Count	Push Pull	Dump Link	Data Document	Electronic Paper	
1 Tbl1	SQL Server 2008 R2	Customer Details	6000123	Customer ID	140	...	Where Country = USA		2345890	Pull	Link	Data	Electronic		
2 File1	Flat File	Product Details	239898	Product ID	120	...	Where Product Category in (x, y, z)		79000	Push	Dump	Data	Electronic		
3 XLS1	Spreadsheet...	Order Details	234865934	Order ID	100	...	All		234865934	Pull	Link	Data	Electronic		
4 jpg1	Jpg file	Product Pictures	123000	Prod_Pic ID	5000		Where Product Category in (x, y, z)		67000	Push	Dump	Document	Electronic		
5 ...															

Fig 2.2.19 Source Data Summary

2. Source Data Relationship:
   Provides relationship between various sources (like an E-R diagram with foreign keys) shown below:

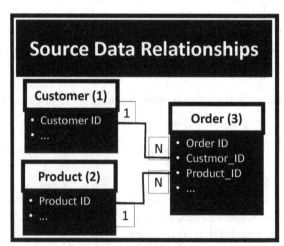

Fig 2.2.20 Source Data Relationships

3. Source Data Details:
   Provide details of all fields from each source.

   An example is shown below:

Source Data Details											
Source ID	Field ID	Field Name	Description	To Migrate	Field Type	Starting Position	Field Length	Min Value	Max Value	Allowed Values	Decimals Places	Comments
1	1	Cust_Name	Customer Name	Y	Text		30					
1	2	Gender	Male or Female	Y	Text		1			M, F		
1	3	Age		N								
1	...											
2	2	Product_Price	Price Per Item	Y	Numeric	120	10	0			2	
2	...											

Fig 2.2.21 Source Data Details

Data Transformation (T)

Data Transformation is a major stage within the ETL process that provides various checks and transformations of data after it gets extracted and before the consolidation is ready to load to the target.

Diagram below shows major processes followed by details during Data Transformation. A sub-set of these processes may be implemented during data migration based upon requirements.

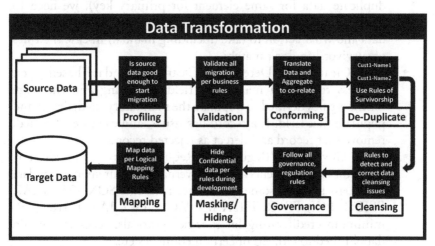

Fig 2.2.22 Data Transformation

Data Transformation contains the following major processes:

- Data Profiling–Data profiling includes viewing the input source for any patterns to judge any exceptions and thus the reliability of the incoming data. As an example, if we expect gender ratio of a country to be within (45% to 55%) range when the total number of records are > 100 million but the range is beyond that, should we use that data or ignore it until its quality becomes reasonable?
- Data Validation – Data validation is performed using business rules that the incoming data should pass including data type, range, allowed values, size, referential integrity and more complex rules. This may need reference to other data sources as well.
- Data Conforming – Various data sources refer to foreign keys (reference keys) for the joins to work and must capture the data at the same level of granularity.
    - o   As an example, if one source refers to country as 'U.S.A' and another source refers to the same country as 'USA', they must be converted (translated) to a common symbol before they can be joined.
    - o   Similarly, if one source includes data at the country level and the other source contains data at the state level, the data at state level must be aggregated at country level before the two sources can be collaborated.
- Data De-duplication – If multiple sources (or one source) contain duplicate data for same element (or primary key), we need to define rules of survivorship, that is, which one to keep in the target data and what action to take (including manual) in case the rules of survivorship don't match?
- Data Cleansing – Detect and Clean up the data based upon business rules. If a mandatory field is missing and there are business rules defined to populate the mandatory field, detect and populate that field. If a record has issues, and can't be corrected, remove that record and detect as rejected record.
- Data Governance/Regulatory Requirements – Provide any regulatory requirements and IT governance requirements that data must pass through some governance rules like SOX 404, GAAP, FFIEC, PCI, ITAR, HIPAA, PPACA, ISO, IAS, EAR, FAR, minimum credit rating for specific approvals, access to certain data limited to citizens of certain countries etc.
- Data Hiding/Masking – For data confidentiality, critical pieces of data may be hidden and replaced with dummy data during various stages (such as testing/development and mock runs). As an example, in some countries, the name of the person may need to be masked

during mock runs. All masking can be done by replacing those values with some dummy values (e.g. *** is used for passwords).

- Data Mapping – This is the major piece and defines how each target data element is derived from various data sources including any transformation logic.

It will include details about all data sources with ways to identify last data converted so that, we can identify what data has changed to avoid duplicate data conversion next time, as well as it allows for dynamic data conversion.

This will also allow pre-collaboration of the data for data fusion so that data that needs collaborated sources is consolidated before it gets mapped with the rest of data sources.

We will also maintain rules to check for completeness of the consolidated target data and check for data completion of the target data.

Here's a simple example for logical data mapping:

Logical Data Map							
Target Details				**Source Details**			
Target Table	Target Field	Table Type (Fact/Dimension)	SCD Type (1, 2, 3,..)	Source Data	Source Field	Transformation Rules	
Customer Table	Full_Name	...	...	Customer File	First Name	Full Name = "First Name"	
				Customer File	Last Name	Full Name = Full_Name & " " & "Last Name"	
Customer Table	Total_Assets	...	N/A	Bank1_Country1	Assets1	Total_Assets = Assets1 * Currency1	
				Bank1_Country2	Assets2	Total_Assets = Total_Assets + Assets2 * Currency2	
				...	...	...	
...	...			...	...	...	

Fig 2.2.23 Logical Data Map

It may be better to normalize these i.e. create a separate table for Target Details with an ID for table and Fields, as well as sources and then just map those IDs and transformation rules.

In reality, we may also need the Physical Data Map that defines how to push/pull the data from source to target including how to access and where are they located and how to transfer data.

Data Loading (L)

Main purpose of data loading is to load the consolidated data after extracting and transforming and ensure its accuracy.

One of the ways to confirm the accuracy is by Data Reconciliation i.e.

- Data Reconciliation – The purpose is to make sure that no incoming data was dropped or duplicated in the migration process by mistake. This can be achieved by various simple or complex ways.

  One simple way, the count check works by keeping record of - the total number of records in the source data, how many were not migrated, how many were rejected and how many were stored in the target data, i.e.

  Total Records Stored in Target should be = Total Records from all Sources – Total Records Not Selected for migration - Total number of records rejected

  Besides Count, we can also choose a value (like an important amount) and sum it up for the same records and totals should also match.

Chapter 2.2.9. Data Migration Quality

The data migration is performed using multiple test runs (aka mock runs), where we may add more and more data sources for each subsequent mock run or repeat the same data sources; and update the software/tools/ infrastructure each time to improve the quality.

One of the biggest challenge, is how to objectively measure the quality of migrated data and then ensure it gets quantitatively improved over time.

How do we ensure that Mock Run 'n+1' is quantitatively better than Mock Run 'n' based upon customer/business requirements?

Typically, we use ticket/issue tracking as the major factor in deciding progress over time. Tickets depend upon internal testing parameters, environment, and the amount of data being captured and not directly related to customer/business requirements.

We are suggesting a data-driven approach to track quantitative improvement over time using 4 major factors i.e.

Confidence Level, Rejection Rate, Performance Level, and Capacity Level based upon business rules defined by the customer/business requirements – explained below

1. **Confidence Level:**
   For each record, identify all potential issues and for each issue define its relative criticality

   As an example, missing SSN (Social Security Number) may be more critical (let's say relative criticality factor 5) than if invoice date < order date (let's assume criticality factor is 3) and so on.

   We add criticality for all issues during data migration to provide **Actual Criticality** during a mock run. Let's assume the sum of all critical issues for a mock run is 1 million.

   Let's say maximum average expected score per record is 10 and total number of records is 1 million, then 10 * 1 Million = 10 Million is the **Maximum Criticality** for that mock run.

   Confidence level =
   *(Maximum Criticality – Actual Criticality)/(Maximum Criticality) * 100 %*

   Confidence Level = (10*1,000,000 – 1,000,000)/(10*1,000,000) = 90%

   (Lowest value for confidence level is 0% i.e. even if the value comes negative) i.e. if the total count of actual issues is more than 10 million, although confidence level computed is negative, we will call it as zero i.e. we have a long way to have a reasonable confidence level, or increase the maximum expected average score per record.

   Purpose of Confidence level - its value should increase over mock runs

   Shown below are some categories/examples of critical factors for confidence level issues but still based upon customer/business needs

   Category1: Self-dependent attribute values where the criticality can be measured just based upon single attribute value such as:
   - Type mismatch
   - Mandatory Field Missing
   - Out of Range of fixed values
   - Field Size

- Checksum Error
- Invalid format
- Not one of allowed values
...

Category2: Depend upon multiple attribute values within same record such as:
- Attribute1 must be <= Attribute2 i.e. Net Salary should be <= Gross Salary
- Attribute2 is Mandatory if Attribute1 has a specific value (If married, Gender is mandatory)
...

Category3: Depends upon attributes across multiple records within same entity (table) such as:
- Duplicate records
- Max records allowed for a type - profiling (Males/Females should be within 45%-55%...) if the total count is > HIGH VALUE
...

Category4: Depends upon attributes across multiple entities (or tables) such as
- Duplicate records across tables
- Referential integrity (if an account activity refers to a customer ID, that customer ID must be valid and must exist)
- Sum of all detail records (count or money) should be same as these totals in corresponding Summary Record
...

Category5: Depends upon Historic Pattern:
- Value of Revenue should be within 10% of the same value from last year record
....

With business rules defined and data captured, it' very easy to automatically compute the confidence level for each mock run.

2. **Rejection Rate:**
   If a record can't be migrated due to any reason (non-numeric data to numeric data type) and it gets rejected, it's calculated as

Rejection Rate = Records Rejected/Total Number of Records *100 %

Purpose is to reduce the rejection rate over mock runs

3. **Performance Level:**
   Let's say the final production run to migrate all data must be completed over a weekend (say 48 hours).

   Let's say based upon time taken for the current mock runs (and its volume and certain other factors), the total expected time to migrate entire data over desired weekend would be 96 hours.

   Then Performance Level = 48*100/96 = 50%

   i.e. Total Required Time Available * 100/Total Expected Time

4. **Capacity Level:**
   Let's say the Total capacity needed for the final migration is 10 Terabyte.

   Let's say based upon the Target Data capacity for current Mock Run (and certain other factors), the total expected final target data capacity would be 7 Terabytes.

   Then Capacity Level = 7 * 100/10= 70%

   i.e. Total Expected Capacity * 100/Total Required Capacity

There could be additional factors such as number of tickets, customer feedback and others…

Overall measurement can be derived based upon all factors and their relative weightage like:

   (100 - Rejection Rate) * Weightage1 * (Confidence Level * Weightage2) …

Although this example refers to Data Migration, this concept can apply to any testing

Chapter 2.2.10. Data Sync-up (Data Bridging) – Only for Legacy Data Migration

Let's assume that due to the complexity and volume of application migration, the application migration is decided to be completed in multiple phases. After a phase, some applications reside in the old system and some in the new system.

Since some applications are still existing in the old system and some have been migrated to the new system, both the old system and the new system are working in parallel.

As example1, let's say the master table maintenance application (like Customer Table) is not migrated in a specific phase but related transaction table maintenance application (like Orders Table) has been migrated. If a new record gets added to master table in the old application, no transaction can be added to the new system related to that master record. Therefore, data updates for master record have to be migrated regularly from the Source to Target Data until master table maintenance gets migrated. This is aka Forward-Bridging.

As example2, let's say the master table maintenance application is migrated in a specific phase but related transaction table maintenance application has not been migrated. If a new record gets added to master table in the new application, no transaction can be added to the old system related to that master record. Therefore, data updates for master record have to be migrated from the Target to Source Data until transaction table maintenance gets migrated. This is aka Backward-Bridging.

Implementation of Forward-Bridging is a bit easier and we can leverage a sub-set of the same tools being used for data migration. Implementation of Backward-Bridging is much more difficult since knowledge of the old application, resources, and tools may be limited, plus we may have to build those applications that may not exist. The common way to implement backward-bridging is by dumping the required master table fields (periodically) to a flat file compatible with old application and add a tool to the old application to import data from the dump file and update the master data.

If possible, best way to migrate all related master and transactional tables and applications in the same phase and if both can't be migrated, then try to migrate the transaction tables maintenance first and the master table maintenance in later phases to avoid backward-bridging.

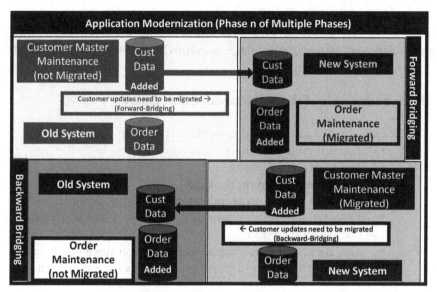

Fig 2.2.24 Application Modernization

Chapter 2.2.11. Business Intelligence

Main purpose of Data Warehousing (consolidated data) is to analyze the data, find some patterns from history for specific conditions and use that as an input to decide what to do next. That is accomplished by Business Intelligence which provides various reports, dashboards, graphs, and other form of text, data, or pictorial output based upon user input. Although business intelligence works primarily on data warehouse, it can also analyze input from other forms of data as well.

In short, business intelligence uses historic and current data to predict the future based upon various business rules, processes, applications, technologies, tools, logic, and user input. Business Intelligence worked primarily on structured data until Big Data came into picture and that will be covered later under Big Data and Business Analytics. Structured data refers to data where its format is pre-defined whereas unstructured data is not pre-defined (like videos, audios, tweets, social media blogs, IoT streams etc.).

For any application (market investment, resolution of medical issues, sales/pre-sales based upon past delivery, risk management, best route to take to reach a destination, and many more), using historic patterns and various requirements as the base, business intelligence can provide useful best solutions.

BI can use the dimension tables to consolidate related data from Fact Table and use the OLAP tools to provide business intelligence reports like How many Product1 items were sold across defined dates/stores/locations and achieved profitability etc.

Here's an example of the importance of Dashboard.

Let's say you are going to unknown far off place in your car.
- You lost your directions
- You have no cell phone
- There are no signs on the road
- Your fuel indicator/car indicators stopped working
- Kids are shouting to stop and take rest while your spouse doesn't want to stop
- You are scared that a cop might catch you since you have no idea what speed you are going and what's the speed limit

What if the car is your company and you are the leader?

You will get all information if your car dashboard works and provides you all analysis and reports.

Chapter 2.2.12. Data Mining

Main purpose of Data Mining is to use patterns of large data sets and use artificial intelligence/machine learning and statistics to provide outcome that can be used for business.

Let's say a company X buys/sells multiple companies and since those companies are not directly related, each works independently. Each company buys the same base products (like paper, steel, gas...) from same or different suppliers/vendors with a short-term contract. If we want to save big money by analyzing all expenses/vendor patterns and then have a long-term contract with a small number of vendors, we can save a good percentage (say 10% of total expense of 5 billion dollars). This is normally called Strategic Sourcing.

Data Mining is one of the methods to analyze the current patterns before deciding which goods to use for Strategic Sourcing and from which vendors and then re-negotiate with proper vendors and finalize the action.

Let's say one of the products sold has the word 'HP', it could mean a computer/printer via Hewlett Packard or it could mean a Motor where HP stands for Horse Power. Therefore, a good degree of pattern search needs to be done before coming up with a decision.

Credit Rating, providing a score etc. based on past history to predict the future is another example of Data mining

Although there are many ways to describe Data Mining, at a high level we are covering six major areas associated with Data Mining i.e.:

1. Classification

Classification is dividing data patterns into discrete and pre-defined categories – employees into specialties, matter into elements, dogs into breeds, people into races, stocks into risks etc. and various other categories

Here are some examples of Classification:
* Classifying credit applications as low, medium, or high risk
* Determining which stocks have better returns and low risks (High, Low, Medium)
* Categorizing employees into skills, experience range, levels, races, professional connectivity (High/Medium/Low LinkedIn), social connectivity (High/Medium/Low Facebook)
* Choosing content to be displayed on a web page into various pre-defined categories
* Determining which phone numbers correspond to fax numbers
* Categorizing politicians into pre-defined winning categories
* Spotting fraudulent insurance claims into various pre-defined categories
* ...

2. Estimation

Whereas classification deals with discrete and pre-defined outcomes (like Low, Medium, High), estimation deals with continuously values outcomes. Given input data, estimation comes up with a value for some unknown continuous variable such as income, Percentage Rating, Credit Rating Score, height, or credit card balance

Here are some examples of Estimation
* Number of children in a family

- Expected Salary of an Employee
- Family household income
- Lifetime value of a customer
- Probability that someone will respond to a survey
- ...

3. Prediction

Same as classification/estimation (Discrete or Continuous) except that the records are classified based upon predicted future behavior

Here are some examples of Prediction
- Predicting size of the balance that will be transferred to credit card
- Predicting the Return and Risk of a market investment
- Which customer will leave a plan within next 6 months?
- Which customers will subscribe to an add-on offer?
- Predicting the next year (or years) revenue of a company
- ...

4. Affinity Grouping

Task of affinity grouping determine which items are co-related and that information can be used for sales/delivery. This can be helpful in finding the arrangement of items on store shelves

Here are some examples of Affinity Grouping
- When a customer buys printer, the probability is high that they buy the paper and thus they should be kept close to each other
- Probability of buying chair mat with chair
- ...

5. Clustering

Classification groups items into pre-defined classes whereas the clusters are not pre-defined for clustering. The clustering takes all objects in a data and groups them into clusters where each cluster contains at least one instance and the total number of clusters <= number of total items.

Here are some examples of Clustering
- There are a large number of projects within a company and you want to cluster those projects in such a way that all projects within

a cluster are considered to be intra-related whereas different clusters may be considered as inter-related

- ...

6. Description and Profiling

Description and Profiling is based upon grouping various elements and describe their behavior and judge the next action based upon their profile. One important factor for profile may be the governance rules.

Here are some examples of Description and Profiling

- A politician may decide profile of the voters based upon their gender, age, race and other profile and act accordingly
- The security check at an airport may be decided based upon individual's profile
- Even a police officer may act based upon the race of an individual
- ...

Chapter 2.2.13. Big Data

What's Big Data?

Let's say we want to review all phone conversations around the world in real-time and report any suspicious activities.

Here's what that requires:

- Collect all the patterns we need to check that may represent suspicious activities
- Collect 100's of millions (or more) of real-time conversations going on around the globe
- Parse the conversations in real time for those patterns (or combinations)
- Build business rules that we need to add to the patterns (such as participant's profiles, location etc.) before defining the suspicious probability
- Define business rules identifying when to report an incident to appropriate authority and act accordingly
- Get a filtered much smaller conversation that may contain those patterns based upon the business rules
- Associate set of patterns and other rules to find the probability

- All these activities must be completed within a very short duration before those suspicious activities turn into real actions
- All these activities must be processed based upon all governance/ regulation rules as to what type of checks can be performed

Big Data has 4 basic important factors (aka 4 V's) called Volume, Velocity, Variety, and Veracity i.e.:

Volume:

Until about 10-15 years back, all of the raw data was manually captured into data repositories and therefore the volume of data was quite finite.

Then came the capture of sensor data (like camera, scanner, or even more complex sensors) where data could be automatically gathered. Even behavioral data captured can be huge - like what web sites an individual is going through and what that may indicate (e.g. looks and books).

The sensor data and behavioral data enhanced the volume exponentially. Same is true for the amount of data in the above example.

This is how the data volumes are measured i.e.:

Kilo, Mega, Giga, Tera, Peta, Exa, Zetta, Yotta, Bronto, Geop

Where 1 Kilo is close to 1000 (actually 2^{10} or 1024) and each next unit gets multiplied by 1024 i.e.

Kilo Byte: 1024^1 i.e. ~10^3
Mega Byte: 1024^2 i.e. ~10^6
Giga Byte: 1024^3 i.e. ~10^9
Tera Byte: 1024^4 i.e. ~10^{12}
Peta Byte: 1024^5 i.e. ~10^{15}
Exa Byte: 1024^6 i.e. ~10^{18}
Zetta Byte: 1024^7 i.e. ~10^{21}
Yotta Byte: 1024^8 i.e. ~10^{24}
Bronto Byte: 1024^9 i.e. ~1027
Geop Byte: 1024^{10} i.e. ~10^{30}

Velocity:

Typical use of data warehousing is to capture the data periodically and use it for periodic decision analysis – like analyze annual/quarterly reports, daily analysis of some sales.

In the example above, all analytic activities must be completed within a very short duration before those conversations turn into suspicious activities.

Therefore, besides the Volume of Data, its Velocity (speed) is also important.

Variety:

All of the data in data warehousing is structured i.e. defined format and captured accordingly in the Fact and Dimensional tables.

When people talk - the format of the conversation, or when a picture of any item is taken – it's pictorial structure, same is true for behavioral data although some of the sensor data can still be structured. Data can also be Semi-Structured such as data captured in various Log Files or some audited data.

In short, BIG Data has a variety of data (Structured, Unstructured, Semi-Structured, or Binary) that includes databases, voice, video, multimedia, sensors including IoT (Internet of Things), emails, social media that is also categorized in 3 types i.e. (Business Data like databases, Machine Data like sensor data, and Human Data like Social/Behavioral Data)

Veracity:

The result of a data warehouse is authentic i.e. if we say we sold 100 items of product1 at store1 for day1 that is real.

Veracity refers to lack of certainty of the data authenticity i.e. level of confidence in its accuracy. If the source of data capture is not authentic, the level of confidence can be low.

Volume, Velocity, Variety, and Veracity are 4 major V's of Big Data although there can be many more V's like Value, Variability, Visualization…

BIG Data – HOW?

There are two important aspects of how to analyze big data i.e. how to store it (Storage) and how to process it (Processing).

First of all, the activities (like conversations) are going on all around the world at multiple locations. Therefore, big data is typically distributed (like on a cloud). One of the common tools associated with BIG data storage is called **HDFS** or Hadoop Distributed File System.

How can we process big data? One of the common processes is MAP Reduce where we send the Query to data instead of data to query (If a sudden major disease occurs in a location, do we send patients to hospital or doctors to that location?)

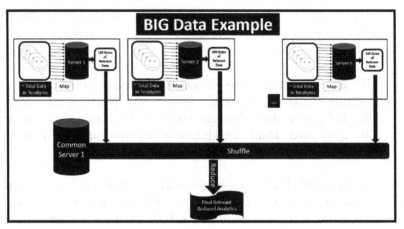

Fig 2.2.25 Big Data Example

- Filter huge amount of data across distributed servers based on business rules
- Consolidate the results from multiple servers (Shuffle) at a common server
- Filter the data (conversations of importance) i.e. REDUCE
- Analyze the patterns and business rules to report any results

For fast response, Big Data may use Column Based Data

What is Column Based Data?

Let's say we want to keep the contact details on a paper notebook. Typical approach (aka Row-Based data) is:

- Page 1 contains Name, address, email, etc. for person1, page 2 for person2 and so on
- Since a human eye can view (buffer) only one page at a time, when you need to get details for an individual go to that page and get full details
- Let's say we want to send an email to all the contacts, we will need to pull each page in our memory (buffer), extract the email part and repeat the same for all contacts
- What if we have millions (or billions) of contacts?

Column Based approach:

- Page 1 contains Names for all contacts, page2 contains address for all contacts, page 3 contains email address for all contacts and so on...
- Let's say we want to send an email to all the contacts, we will need to pull only page3 in our memory (buffer) and then filter if we need to send to only a subset of contacts
- It's easier to keep data for different attributes on separate servers providing better velocity, plus we can maintain columns in real-time
- However, if we need all fields for just one contact, it's the other way around i.e. in row-based data, we can get that all attributes for one person in a single access, whereas in column-based data, we may need to scan multiple pages

    If we need to retrieve many rows but few columns, Column-based approach is much better. If we need few rows but multiple columns, Row-based approach is better.

Besides Column based, the data can even be stored by Column Store i.e.

Let's say we have 1000 persons, all of them have names and their IDs (like Social Security Number in the US), but only 500 have addresses, 700 have family details, 800 have emails and so on.

Since each column data is stored separately in Column Based data, Columns for Names and Social Security numbers contain 1000 entries, Column for Addresses contains only 500 entries, for Family Details 700 entries, and Emails only 800 entries.

Overall it optimizes the storage, provides much better speed if only few columns (out of many) are needed, and each column can be maintained on separate storage if needed.

Big Data Analogy?

We believe a human being is an excellent example of a Big Data machine i.e.:

- Our eyes are not meant for viewing only one type of data but have multiple servers that view all types of data. Same is true for our ears and nose...
- Our Eyes, Ears, and Nose Map Data, shuffle it, and Reduce it and send to Brain for Brain Analytics based upon various business rules
- Moreover, all processing is memory (human-memory) based
- For supercomputers, distance between CPU and input peripherals is a major issue since even light takes 1 nanosecond to travel 30 cm
- Eyes, Ears, and Nose are major input peripherals and are very close to the brain
- Let's say we see a moving car with open door in front of us, we capture just that information from the car (like column-store) and no other attributes or other countless views
- All incoming data gets filtered (Map Reduced) by eyes/ears/nose before it's analyzed by the brain (Brain Analytics), then the Brain decides what to do next i.e. for the car with open door, the brain can even take the action and inform the driver of the car about the open door

The Big Data and even the Cognitive machines capture and analyze data to suggest (don't act) a next best action, whereas a human being can also take action.

There are two main ways to cover processing i.e.

Even though the data is distributed, we can process it by smaller number of distributed servers but they have much more complex hardware (including high degree of memory), or a large number of distributed but much simpler and less complex servers. Each has its Pros/Cons.

Two of common methods are based upon these two strategies. Hadoop is based upon less complex but more number of servers whereas SAP Hana is based upon more complex but less quantity (memory-based) of hardware.

Big Data is used for Static Data (based upon data captured), or Dynamic Data (like real-time streaming) i.e. data-in-motion vs. data-at-rest. Real Time Analytic Processing (RTAP) is used for dynamic data.

Data Wrangling is used to capture data for proper use and involves 4 main steps:

1. Capture Storage on cloud
2. Create columns to classify/distinguish data. Even if there's no data portion available that can define uniqueness for the data, only one incident can occur at one place at one instant. Therefore, it can capture x, y, z location (via geolocation) and time as the unique key
3. Normalize the data close to 1st Normal Form
4. Apply analytics to add value

Information Virtualization is used to provide results that include two main layers of services i.e.:

1. Info delivery: Via Interfaces and APIs using Metadata
2. Info provisioning: Via Caching (in memory for fast processing), Federation (Real time but not consistent), Consolidation (Consistent but not real time), and Replication (Read-only copy)

Chapter 2.2.14. Data Lakes

Normally data from various sources is analyzed and consolidated, whereas in Data Lakes original data is retained in their own natural format. It allows to keep all original data and avoid delay of processing the data.

The type of data in a data lake could be structured, un-structured, semi-structured or binary data. Typically, each data lake is uniquely identified based upon data or if no unique data identification is available it's geolocation (x, y, z co-ordinates of where data is collected) and when (time) is used to identify its uniqueness, since only one thing can happen at a given time at a given location.

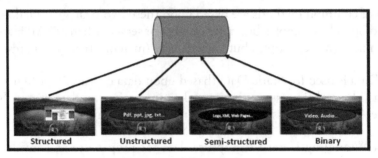

Fig 2.2.26 Data Lakes

Chapter 2.2.15. Business Analytics

Once Big data is captured, the process to analyze for business purpose is called Business Analytics and has 4 major types i.e.:

Descriptive Analytics (with Diagnostic): To describe a pattern based upon historical data and treat exceptions (diagnostics) separately.

Predictive Analytics: To predict what is expected to happen in the future based upon historic patterns.

Prescriptive Analytics: To prescribe what action to take based upon predictive analytics and other realistic information i.e. what's recommended.

Cognitive Analytics: Cognitive computing combines artificial intelligence and machine-learning algorithms, in an approach which attempts to reproduce the behavior of human brain and makes it better over experience, since it makes the system learn as it does the job.

The purpose of a cognitive machine is to get smarter and more customized through interactions with data, devices and people, and the purpose of Cognitive Analytics tools is to simulate Human Cognition through Cognitive Machines. It uses knowledge, attention, memory, judgment, evaluation, reasoning, and computation – for problem solving and decision making.

Cognitive machines can simulate Help Desks, Health Care, Financial, and various other areas.

Here's an example of Descriptive (with Diagnostic), Predictive, Prescriptive, and Cognitive Analytics:

Let's say we want to invest in the Stock Market with High Returns with Low Risk based upon their probability.

Let's use 3 different types of data i.e.

1. All market data i.e. for all desired equities, keep track of their quotes, volumes, dividends, stock splits etc.
2. For each equity (stock, ETF, Mutual Fund…), use large number of strategies i.e. when to buy and when to sell.

> Here's an example of one Strategy: Place an order to buy at 99% of reference price for 2 days. Reference price could be today's opening price, last business day's closing price, or last time we sold that equity). If not able to buy after 2 days, change it to 99.5% and wait for another 10 days, if still not able to buy, place an order to buy at next day's opening price.

> Once bought, place the order to sell like: sell at 101% of purchase price, wait for n1 days, if not sold, place the order to sell at 100.5 for n2, days, if not sold at 100 for n3 days, if not sold for defined days of waiting, then sell at next day opening price to minimize risk of further loss.

> One can define any number of strategies for each equity. Moreover, let the system automatically choose various strategies based upon various factors for an equity. Here's a pictorial way to show a strategy:

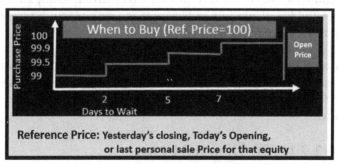

Fig 2.2.27 When to Buy

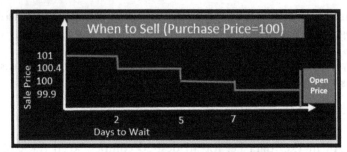

Fig 2.2.28 When to Sell

3. Define many ways to compute the risk for an equity, or equity/ strategy....

Based upon this data, provide analytics based upon various patterns and requirements like relative importance of risk and return, type of equities and so on. That portion covers **Descriptive Analytics.**

Let's say due to a total market crash on a particular day, the entire analytics was impacted that day. We can consider that as part of **Diagnostic Analytics** and keep those exceptions separate and provide analytics without those exceptions.

We can provide what returns, and risks we expect in the future based upon various data patterns. That will cover **Predictive Analytics.**

How accurate is our Predictive Analytics? We can analyze that based upon certain other business rules and future expectations to cover what we prescribe i.e. **Prescriptive Analytics.** Another important way to prescribe could be – look at all the past and for each period (say quarter), analyze what would have been our prediction based upon the data prior to that quarter and what was the real results for that quarter. Compare those for all equities and for all quarters and use that as a major input for prescriptive analytics to be more realistic.

We can also simulate a Cognitive Machine that can auto track the past, present, and future and understand the customer's mindset and simulate the stock market investment on his/her behalf using **Cognitive Analytics.**

Chapter 2.2.16. Big Data and Cloud

Since big data is distributed across multiple data nodes with potential real-time processing, big data is distributed over the cloud.

Here's a future big data/cloud potential idea:

Let's put sensors on human being like:

1. A sensor for the eyes that captures all the pictures (n pictures/ second) that the person is watching in real-life and automatically stores on the cloud. Moreover, we can even include backward pictures or from other angles. Backward pictures can be viewed even in real-life regardless of cloud, just like a car normally has reverse mirror(s)
2. A sensor for the ears that captures all the audio that the person is listening in real-life and automatically captures on the cloud
3. A sensor for the mouth that captures all the audio that the person is speaking in real-life and automatically captures on the cloud

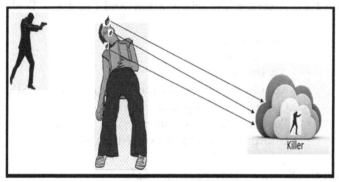

Fig 2.2.29 Future Big Data and Cloud Potential Idea

For complete security, the sensor can capture some uniqueness within the human body (like DNA ID) and each data is captured using that DNA ID and can be accessed again only by using the same DNA ID i.e. the person can analyze all the data. Some locations can authorize the cloud server company to disable the data capture while customers are located in that location for security purpose.

Moreover, the person can authorize if someone else can use a portion of the data using his/her DNA ID – as an example, if a person gets killed, the spouse or other family members can view the details, share subset with proper authorities (like police) and find out details about the person's death. This can reduce the probability of crimes.

Of course, this can provide great business and the pricing may depend upon various factors including the value of 'n' pictures/unit.

Chapter 2.2.17. Common Tools/Technologies related to Data:

Common RDBMS (Relational Data Base Management System):

- Oracle Database
- Microsoft SQL Server
- MySQL (Oracle Corporation)
- IBM DB2
- IBM Informix
- Teradata
- SAP Sybase Adaptive Server Enterprise
- SAP Sybase IQ

Common ETL (Extract, Transformation, and Loading) Tools:

- Informatica
- Data Stage
- AB Initio
- Microsoft SQL Server Integration Services (SSIS)
- Oracle Data Integrator
- Pentaho Data Integration
- Information Builders Data Migrator

Common BI (Business Intelligence) Tools:

- Pentaho BI
- MicroStrategy
- Microsoft SQL Server Analysis Services (SSAS)
- Microsoft SQL Server Reporting Services (SSRS)
- R Language
- SAP Business Objects Data Integrator
- Oracle Business Intelligence Enterprise Edition (OBIEE)
- Oracle Hyperion System
- QlikView/QlikSense/Tableau
- Yellowfin BI
- SiSense
- Cognos

Common Data Mining Tools:

- Mahout

- Weka
- RapidMiner
- KNIME
- Rattle

Chapter 2.2.18. Tools/Technologies for Big Data:

Here are some details covering some common technologies/tools used in Hadoop.

Storage

HDFS (Hadoop Distributed File System):

Provides a distributed file system where the data is kept in multiple Data Nodes (aka Daemon Slave Data Nodes).

Same data is replicated in multiple nodes (3 fault tolerant data nodes by default), so that even if some data nodes are not available, it's copy can be used to retrieve the data.

The content (like Table of Contents) of data nodes is maintained in a Name Node. In the initial phase of Hadoop (version 1.0), there was no backup of Name node whereas in version 2.0 (aka Yarn), a copy of Name Node is maintained.

Data is kept in reasonable memory (or Chunks/blocks) of 64/128 Mega Bytes.

Besides the storage, even jobs are distributed into Tasks and various tasks are kept under Task Trackers and their status is maintained in Job Tracker. Multiple tasks are processed in parallel using MPP (Massive Parallel Processing).

HDFS uses Java as the base language.

HBase – noSQL where no SQL may stand for Not Only SQL (Structured Query Language), or Non-Relational SQL.

HBase is like a database whereas HDFS is a file system. Although there are some technical differences between the two of them, main purpose of both is to provide distributed storage for Hadoop data.

HBase is also using Java as the language.

Hive: To help existing users of RDBMS, Facebook provided Hive that supports SQL like language called Hive SQL (HQL) where Hadoop's summarized HDFS data is provided in a Hive Data warehouse.

Hive is quite slow, batch-based and allows only to append data that is not ACID (Atomicity, Consistency, Isolation, Durability)

Interfacing with other (non-Hadoop) data repositories to collect data:

Hadoop Products:

> **Sqoop:** Exports RDBMS data to HDFS and vice-versa. If data is maintained in common RDBMS like Oracle or Microsoft SQL, Sqoop can be used to import data from them to Hadoop or export from Hadoop to RDBMS.

> **Flume:** Gets data stream from systems like Twitter or other IOT (Internet Of Things). It uses Message Queues type process to use all data logs from other systems as a base to populate that data to Hadoop and uses streaming data flow.

Besides Hadoop, Other products provide tools to interface with Hadoop like:

SAP Hana provides Vora that uses Spark as a base to interface with Hadoop and RDBMS

Collaboration across multiple Hadoop Products:

> **Apache Oozie:** Manages workflow across various Hadoop products i.e. what to do and when based upon various factors. Operations are done via sub-commands Command Line Interface (CLI)

> **Apache ZooKeeper:** Synchronizes data/apps across various products with a control over deadlock and race conditions. Also, provides APIs to Create, Get, Update, Delete. Part of Hadoop version 2.0. A distributed process management system.

Ambari: Provides provisioning, managing, and maintenance of various Hadoop Clusters

Apache Hadoop is Open Source whereas there are many related products like Cloudera, Hortonworks, and MapR that are commercial). Hortonworks uses Microsoft Windows Azure as the base for their cloud, and Cloudera uses Hue-UI Framework, and SDK Hue.

There are many products for proper business analytics such as Vertica, Cassandra (both column-based), SAS, Kafka, Netezza, Mongo DB (for document analytics), CouchDB (uses documents as DB), Neo4J (uses Graphics as DB).

Spark/Storm (Open Source) Impala (by Cloudera) are pretty fast and memory-based products for business analytics.

Other products:

Mahout is used for Machine learning algorithm and Data Mining algorithm

Python, R-Language, Perl, Java, Pig Latin, JSON (or BSON) and Scala are most common languages

Pig Latin (by Yahoo) is mainly an ETL product for Big Data

SAP HANA is mainly based on column-store and memory-based machines, provides a faster response using products like TREX, P*Time, MVCC (Multi-version Concurrency Control), and Vora for interfacing with Hadoop and RDBMS).

Sub-Section 2.3

Enterprise Architecture

Whether manually or technology driven, if one asks a question and before we can provide the response, we need mainly 3 layers to respond back as shown in the diagram below:

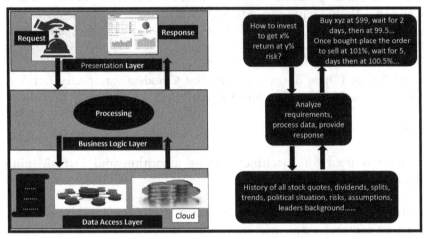

Fig 2.3 Enterprise Architecture

These layers can be implemented using various physical parts called (tiers).

Do we have the proper framework that can integrate across all people, tools, technology, data, communications, locations, and others in real-time so that we can visualize what's happening and act accordingly?

All elements and sub-elements across various layers and tiers need to have means to communicate with each other before proper collaboration can be successful.

As an example, if within a family one wants to co-ordinate, they may need to communicate on a regular basis. In a big global business, a framework/ architecture needs to be created that can ease proper collaboration.

Besides various layers and tiers, the enterprise architecture includes 4 main frameworks i.e.:

1. If there are many people using 10 languages, do we need tools to translate each language to other 9. If so we will need 10*9 = 90 language translation tools.

   Another way could be to use one of them as a common language and find a tool to translate other 9 to the common language and vice-versa i.e. total of 2*9=18 tools. This is similar to Canonical Data Model or Federation model from enterprise architecture perspective. It may have pros (fewer tools) and cons (may need double translation).

2. If person A wants to send a message to person B, do they have to do live talk? If so, both must be present at the same time. Or, other means to send communication and receive it in a queue (like email or voicemail) regardless of their availability. This is similar to Message Queuing from enterprise architecture perspective that includes MQSeries that became WebSphere by IBM, MSMQ by Microsoft, Tuxedo/Q by BEA. Again, it may have pros and cons.

3. If one wants to talk to a specialist, the person may need to talk to a common person to find the best person to talk and then contact details.

   Similarly, when one uses a URL for a site, the actual location of the site (IP address) may be unknown and dynamic. So, it uses DNS (Domain Name Servers) to get the IP address for the URL and then go to that site.

   This is similar to yellow pages and the terms used from technical enterprise architecture point include middleware object, CORBA, and Service Oriented Architecture (SOA) using UDDI (Universal Description, Discovery, and Integration).

4. How to collaborate across various mindsets, cultures, or tools? This is similar to what's called Enterprise Application Interface (EAI) from enterprise architecture perspective to co-relate various applications.

Chapter 2.3.1. Service-Oriented Architecture (SOA):

Normally, all services provided by software are utilized by Application Program Interface (API) i.e. format of the services are pre-defined. If the service interface changes, the program to call that service also needs to be changed.

Service-Oriented Architecture allows the services and their usage to be independent via a 2-step process. In the first step, the service user program asks for a type of service and its interface. In the second step, it calls the service based upon the interface responded in step1. It's just like yellow pages highlighted in the diagram below:

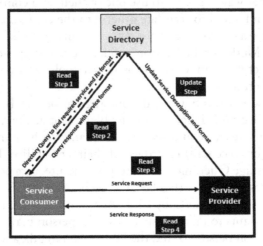

Fig 2.3.1 Service-Oriented Architecture (SOA)

Service is typically called as Web Service, and Web Services Description Language (WSDL) is a format for describing a Web Services interface. This definition is published to a directory of services. Typical directory could be UDDI (Universal Description, Discovery, and Integration).

Chapter 2.3.2. Reference, Target, and Existing Architecture:

- To complete a project, what's desired as the framework from various areas is the Reference Architecture
- What is practical and is decided as the ultimate architecture is called the Target Architecture (To-Be), also sometimes referred at Point of Arrival (PoA)
- What framework is currently present from same areas is called as Existing (As-Is) Architecture, also sometimes referred at Point of Departure (PoD)

Typical areas of framework may include Technology, Business, Process, Information, and Organization.

Refer to the example shown in chapter 1.2.15 (Balance As-Is vs. To-Be scenario)

Chapter 2.3.3. Emerging trends and future-vision architecture:

Owing to cost pressures, many organizations are shifting to open source, to avoid the hefty licensing fees for software. Traditionally applications were built as monolithic, very tightly coupled across modules. While this provided efficiency at the time of its development, as that was all there was in sight then, as the load and usage grew, the monolithic architecture became a bottleneck. There was no reusability across lines of business except for smartly developed reusable code, and performance got slower as number of users increased.

Legacy transformation became a booming business for the IT industry, as most large corporations with a codebase developed about 50 years ago in Cobol, started seeing loss of knowledge base owing to attrition and retirement of those responsible for development. Though legacy code and mainframes on which it is hosted still work great, lack of skilled Cobol consultants and less documentation, started forcing transformation projects.

Instead of being limited, large organizations are embracing modern trends while putting wrappers on, and exposing the legacy code as services through tools like CICS (Customer Information Control System) transaction gateway, leveraging the existing legacy codebase as callable SOA services.

Performance bottlenecks started forcing breakup of monolithic application architectures at the point of break, and resolving the issues independently through a newly emerging concept of Microservices.

Microservices

Microservices are a SOA pattern, focused on achieving a single task well, exposed through an API, can be developed in any language, and are typically designed and developed by smaller teams in an agile environment. Automation is key to success for Microservices, and DevOps is the way to go for achieving continuous integration, testing, and deployment. This enables development of new features and realization of newer releases faster, helping bring new products and services much quicker to market.

What to develop/use when - Business/SOA vs. Microservices

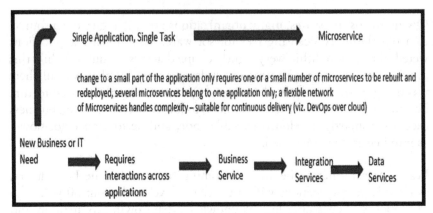

Fig 2.3.2 When to develop a Microservice

Business Services can be composite requiring several integration and data services to reach required applications or systems/databases – orchestration and choreography may be required to put together a comprehensive response, and are typically exposed through a standardized interface through an ESB that is available to multiple consumers.

The Microservices selection dilemma

- The key business drivers for Microservices are doing business at scale, leveraging the cloud environment to enable millions of users reach you through their smart devices and buy – making these ideally suitable for large-scale retail operations on the web, like by leveraging common search product, search inventory, purchase order etc.
- An individual *microservice* is implemented with a single purpose, is self-contained, and independent of other instances and services
- We need to carefully evaluate the interaction with legacy applications, and owing to lack of mediation capabilities with Microservices, it may become limiting in some ways to interact across various applications to achieve execution of any complex functionality with use of just Microservices
- One of the key shifts that would be required is in terms of organization – Microservices paradigm is centered around "You write it, you run it" culture and a "2-pizza" team size

Two Speed IT decision tree

- Microservices are the route to take for single tasks that can be executed independently, providing speed and scale to operations when millions of transactions are likely to hit through customers using multiple Systems of Engagement (SoE, viz. smart devices, tablets)
- Business Services is the route to take for jobs that require interactions between applications (both legacy and modern), needing access to multiple Systems of Record (SoR) and a choreographed orchestration of responses from these SoRs

Microservices are exposed through an endpoint (viz. REST API)

- API refers to any interface that is exposed over REST (HTTP/JSON) or a web service (SOAP/HTTP). The APIs are typically categorized by their scope, such as a public API or an enterprise API
- Service exposure has evolved into APIs, simplifying exposure interface, consumption, management, and, in some cases, monetizing business functions
- New application architectures, including the Microservices architecture, enable developers to focus more closely on business logic, continuously pushing infrastructural detail to the environment in which they run
- The combination of these developments enables solutions to be built in more agile styles and applications to benefit from new levels of elastic scalability and fault tolerance
- The granularity of APIs provided by Microservices is often different than what is needed by a client - Microservices typically provide fine-grained APIs, which means that clients need to interact with multiple services, for example, a client needing details for a product would need to fetch data from numerous services
- Business services, Microservices, APIs are all SOA adoption patterns that fit appropriately by the context in different spaces – we can define what to use when and how by the context and relevance to leverage key business benefits of each
- We can start small and then grow – begin with identifying some key services and the patterns to implement, and learn from experience by failing early
- Typically, Microservices are not to be used until the evolution of a traditionally written application begins to reach an inflexion point of complexity - for this approach to work, we need to write a suitably structured application from the beginning and choose

the right moment to make the transition: one does not start with Microservices to begin with, and takes this route to scale the operations by leveraging cloud elasticity and autonomous, independent automation of Microservices

Emerging towards a culture of loose coupling and reusability

As organizations tend to develop SOA business and integration services, Microservices and APIs, over a period of time these tend to become re-usable Lego blocks, which can be assembled quickly by revising configuration, creating a specific instance of a service for new use as needed.

Take an example of a bank – searching a particular customer and then retrieving account details would be required across all lines of business from retail to wholesale for different account types like savings, checking, term deposits, mortgage, wealth management etc. If the bank introduced a new product, they would leverage the exact same existing services to find the customer and retrieve account details. It becomes possible through loose coupling between application modules, and break up of functionality into smaller, manageable blocks that can be easily managed for development and deployment.

This is similar to a media developer having small reusable cartoon snippets that they can first create an inventory of, and then discover to reuse or adapt from that inventory, instead of reinventing the wheel to create the exact same snippet again.

Thus, from SOA business services to business processes to code snippets to Microservices, are all reusable assets that first need to be put in an enterprise services catalog (service registry) from where these can be found for reuse or adoption. This is all part of the Eco-System evolution of IT landscape for an enterprise – in the target state process, cross-functional/line of business priority use cases driven by business need urgency and value, are mapped to foundational and Information Management (IM) capabilities.

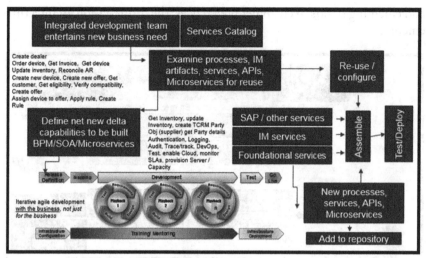

Fig 2.3.3 Towards evolution of the ecosystem
with examples of reusability

Increased decoupling and separation of concerns, like modularizing functionalities of omni-channel access, providing targeted end-user experience to specific customer segments through portlets, business processes, applications, business services, integration services, data access services etc. all lead to emergence of a layered architecture. Such layers can co-exist across infrastructure, network, software, and cloud architectures, and these multi-layered architectures attempt to dissolve the complexity of large projects to understandable, and manageable solution components.

While evolving to the future, successful enterprises tend to decrease their technology debt by rationalizing and consolidating least used applications and data sources to more used existing and in-flight target services, applications/projects, and simultaneously moving away from heavy in-house data center and application development culture. This lowers total cost of ownership (TCO), capital expenditure, and embracing pay by usage cloud deployment or pay by development models, freeing up resources to let the enterprise focus on its business rather than sweat and worry about the IT complexity.

Future-vision Architecture:

As layered architectures evolve, keeping separation of concerns, containing similar functionality within layers, with focus on reusability and creating all net new deltas with reusability in mind across channels, lines of business and emerging trends in customer preferences, the future-vision architecture emerges.

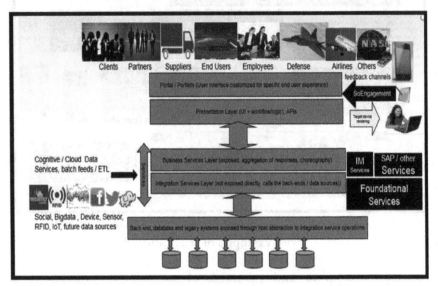

Fig 2.3.4 Example of a simplified future-vision architecture

The future-vision architecture is scalable, adaptable, and akin to grow as does the business. Embracing open standards and industry best practices, yet customized to meet the exacting business needs of the enterprise for which it is designed, leverages key capabilities of the existing systems and infrastructure as far as possible, and keeps adding new systems and technologies as part of the evolution and growth process.

It can accept various types of data from multiple sources, including social, streaming, IoT, sensors, co-exists with existing systems, and adapts new development and deployment trends like Microservices, DevOps, Cloud, and open source.

The key shift here is creating an integrated team that looks beyond the silos and has a sight of business need and growth across and beyond the enterprise, with focus on the end customer and consumer of the products and services.

Sub-Section 2.4

Enterprise Mobility

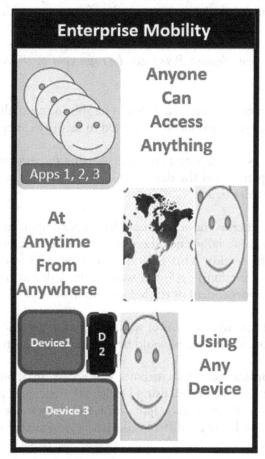

Fig 2.4 Enterprise Mobility

Purpose of 'Enterprise Mobility' is to let

> **Anyone** use
>> **Any Device** at
>>> **Any Time** from
>>>> **Anywhere** to Access
>>>>> **Any Data/Application**

Any Device: Besides laptops or desktop computers, there are many other devices that are connected to the network (direct or via internet) to other devices (like servers).

That includes various cell phones (using different type of software as a base), I Pads, many devices connected to a home or a vehicle, and more may be added.

How about if even Human Being can be connected to the network in the future?

Any device that can be connected should be able to access all the data and tools that can be accessed locally – limited to security concerns.

In other words which device a customer is using to perform any activity should not depend upon the device being used – except if some devices can impact security issues.

Anytime/Anywhere: The access shouldn't depend upon time of the day, or from where (especially since the times could be different at different locations in the world). This is similar to Follow-The-Sun covered in chapter 3.4.8 (Functions) approach where help desk can be provided 24 hours of a day independent of the help location.

Again, if there are any concerns of security issues at a particular time at a specific location, some control could be implemented accordingly.

Any Data/Application: If a customer can access an application and a data from location1, at Time1, using Device D1 – the same person should be able to access the same data/application from any other location, at a different time, and using a different device as long as that doesn't create a security issue.

Sub-Section 2.5

Enterprise Security

As the number of users increases and anyone can use it – security becomes a bigger issue

> As one can use any device – security becomes a bigger issue
> > As one can access at any time – security becomes a bigger issue
> > > As one can access from anywhere – security becomes a bigger issue
> > > > As one can access any data/app – security becomes a bigger issue

Therefore, security will be used to control the access based upon various rules/regulations. Geo-location of the device can also be checked to find appropriate rules for the location.

There are 3 main areas for security management:

1. **Access**: Level/extent of a service, device, functionality, or data that a user is entitled to use or view on a 'need to know basis'
2. **Identity**: Unique name used to identify a user, person, or role. Used to grant rights with a way to authenticate identity such as password, fingerprint (*or DNA in future…*)
3. **Rights** (Privileges): Entitlements or permissions granted to a user/ role. Typical privileges may include: Read/Write/Execute/Change/ Delete – a reviewer or approver of data can only look at data to either return to data creator with comments or approval, but cannot create new records, or update/delete existing ones

Based upon security requirements, one may decide the kind of cloud such as Private/Public/Hybrid Cloud.

Security may also be controlled based upon various regulation/governance rules by various countries.

Organizations can provide procedures, processes, and mechanism to monitor and control the access to data. Private personal identifiers (like social security number, date of birth etc.) are typically masked for viewing to prevent abuse, and encrypted before transmission on a network.

Employees making attempts to access data to which they are not entitled are red-flagged and all such attempts are logged and monitored for filtering accidental breach vs. deliberate efforts with malicious intention. Such logs are like big data that can be mined per defined algorithms.

This whole concept is related to Cybersecurity and Cybercrime. Many companies are actively working on providing security for their data/tools. Please go online or refer to security experts to get more technical details and tools/applications that can provide appropriate security for your needs.

Sub-Section 2.6

Summary of Technical Framework

2.1 Technical Base

- **Hardware:** circuits, memory, processors, and the chassis on which mounted – devices, servers, computers etc.
- **Infrastructure:** collective hardware and networking resources
- **Network:** connections between communication devices like modems, routers, network switches and computing resources through wired or wireless radio medium
- **Software:** programs, utilities, tools, systems, and applications that enable the execution of a given task using computing resources
- **Cloud Computing** (SaaS, PaaS, IaaS, QaaS): as a Service for Software, Platform, Infrastructure, Quality, business processes, solution, database etc. provided in the virtualized, off-premises environment to lower cost of ownership and shift of capital expenditure to operating expenses
- **Virtualization:** sharing of IT infrastructure among many computing resources like servers, dynamically provisioned (or de-provisioned) based on consumer demands
- **IoT** (Internet of Things): Inter-communication between devices and supporting computing resources, like connected car, refrigerator, washing machine, manufacturing machines, airplanes etc. generating data that is interpreted for next best action or procedural step
- **Architecture:** blue-print that lays the foundation for design and development activities
- **Common Tools/Technologies related to Technical Base:** set of open source and supplier-provided applications and resources that enable achievement of specific tasks and fulfillment of business objectives

2.2 Data & Big Data

- **Data Management**: Manage Data and how to convert Data into Information
- **Hierarchical Model**: Only one-many i.e. no record can have more than one master
- **Network Model**: Many-Many
- **Relational Model**: Two-dimensional structure (Rows and Columns) where relationship can be built across any set of Rows and Columns
- **Data Normalization and Modeling**: Normalization provides proper data structure so that data can be added/deleted/updated properly. Modeling provides best ways to model the data to relate various groups of data (Entities/Tables...)
- **Transactional Database**: Data repository to use, mainly for maintaining all processes that include data updates. So, the transactional database needs to be at the lowest level with processing for all transactions
- **Data Warehouse**: Normally a summary of useful data for making decisions. A read-only data repository that gets created periodically from transactional data. Moreover, data is more than two-dimensional
- **ETL (Extraction, Transformation, & Loading) Process**: Way to migrate data from various data sources of old application to new application if the application gets modified. This is typically a one-time process only. Also, used to periodically migrate the data and summarize to populate Data Warehouse from Transactional Data as an operational process
- **Data Migration Quality**: How to ensure that we are making quantitative improvement during various phases of testing for data migration
- **Data Sync-up (Data Bridging)**: In case application gets modified but in multiple phases. Until all phases are complete, both the old system and new system are running in parallel. To make them functional, part of the data needed in the other system may need to be regularly synchronized
- **Business Intelligence**: To analyze the data warehouse and get proper reports
- **Data Mining**: Use patterns of large data sets and use artificial intelligence/ machine learning and statistics to provide outcome that can be used for business.
- **Big Data**: Best way to store and process the data that has very high Volume, need high Speed (Velocity), Variety of data (Structure, Unstructured, Semi-Structured, Binary), and Veracity (lack of certainty of the data authenticity)
- **Business Analytics**: Provides Descriptive (historic patterns), Predictive (future prediction), Prescriptive (Recommended action to take), and Cognitive (Simulate human behavior to machines for various needs based upon data) analytics – using big data

2.3. Enterprise Architecture

- Service-Oriented Architecture (SOA): Provides Services that can be maintained independent of its use and a user first finds the kind of services available based upon their requirements using UDDI (Universal Description, Discovery, and Integration) with the format of the request, and then use that service with the format provided by UDDI to get the result
- Reference, Target, and Existing Architecture: Existing Architecture (Current Condition across various areas), Reference Architecture (Desired Condition across various areas), Target Architecture (Practical agreed Condition across various areas)

2.4. Enterprise Mobility
Anyone can access a system using any device from anywhere, anytime, and from any location

2.5. Enterprise Security
As number of users become more, one can access from anywhere, anytime, and using any device – security becomes a bigger issue

Section 3

Business Framework

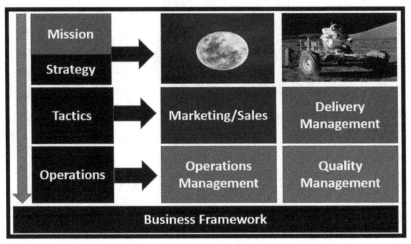

Fig 3.0 Business Framework

Sub-Section 3.1

Accomplish Mission with
Strategy, Tactics, Operations

Mission is related to ultimate goal as decided by the leadership team based upon various factors including their practicality, cost/benefit analysis, and various tangible/intangible factors.

Here are some examples of the mission:

- The mission of this book is to implement whatever is practical for their business to achieve success via Strategic Balancing based upon Factual Data
- A school student may have the mission to become a doctor
- The mission of a car manufacturer may be to reach the rank of world's top 5 manufacturers based upon overall annual revenue and profit in the next 5 years
- The mission of a US president may be to reduce the unemployment rate percentage below 5% over next 5 years
- Mission of the leader of country1 may be to destroy their enemy
- Even the terrorists, or other leaders may have a purpose that may be undesired by the overall community – but even they have a mission

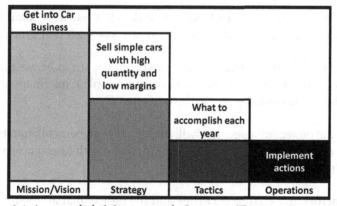

Fig 3.1 Accomplish Mission with Strategy, Tactics, Operations

Once we decide when to accomplish a mission (with high level summary of its purpose and budget), we need to define the Strategy, Tactics, and Operations to accomplish them as highlighted below:

> **Strategy** is based upon the final (or long-term) needs and based more upon desires and quality and less on quantitative measures and analysis.

> **Tactics** are more practical with detailed plans of quantitative requirements and need to be measured, analyzed and next tactics may be adjusted accordingly.

> Once Tactics are planned, we need to implement them via **Operations**.

One example of a mission is covered under Chapter 1.2.15 (Balance As-Is vs. To-Be scenario) covering the mission involved to reach the moon (shown in the diagram above).

To accomplish any mission, we will have multiple areas and sub-areas (like Business Needs, Partnerships, HR Management, Data Management, Infrastructure Management, Communications with Status Sharing, and many more technical, business, social, and other areas).

Main purpose of a business is to synchronize/optimize all areas to achieve the best result for the ultimate mission.

The purpose of strategic leadership is to decide what to accomplish and the project management will deliver that purpose with best productivity.

Once we understand where we are and where we want to be, we may need multiple phases for various areas and define complete roadmaps and how to collaborate them to optimize the outcome.

Finally, the project management will decide - how to best collaborate across various areas and phases to reach the destination with lowest cost and best quality/profitability.

Many factors may change over time and the project management needs to act and adjust accordingly.

Sub-Section 3.2

Sales/Pre-Sales

Once a mission is decided, we might need proper plans to market/sell its outcome.

Sales/Pre-Sales is a complex topic and here are a few important factors to consider:

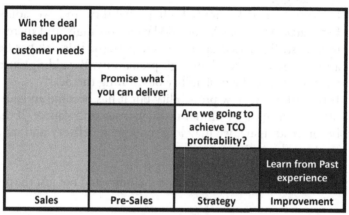

Fig 3.2 Sales/Pre-Sales

Chapter 3.2.1. Balance Sales/Delivery:

It's very important to balance sales/delivery for best profitability so that what we promise, we can deliver. Shown below are 3 important steps:

1. Quotes we provide for any task should not be based just upon discussions with experts, but also based upon historic data i.e. if our subject matter experts think, a task should take 100 hours and we have delivered same (or similar) task many times in the past and has never taken under 500 hours (or vice versa), we should analyze both and try to find how to adjust the effort and then provide a realistic quote
In other words, if the historic effort was 500 hours and the quote is 100 hours, and our realistic current figure comes still to 400 hours – if we still use 100 hours as the base for the quote (underquote), we will lose on delivery and may even have to abort the delivery.

If the historic effort was 100 hours and our quote is 400 hours, but the realistic figure still comes to 200 hours, by quoting 400 hours, we may make more money if we win the deal, but we reduce the probability of winning the deal and if so, we may waste all the money to win the deal (overquote)

2. Ensure what we promise, we are capable of delivering based upon our capabilities, resources and past experience using factual data

3. If we think a risk is high (or low) and price it accordingly, if that risk had been used many times in the past but has rarely (or many times) become an issue, we should adjust the risk probability accordingly.

   Let's say the risk shows high probability and we adjust our Estimated Monitory Value (EMV) accordingly and increase the total cost. But based upon historic patterns this risk has become an issue much lesser than high probability. By adding extra cost, we may reduce the probability of winning the deal.

   If the risk shows low probability but it has become an issue more often in the past for similar tasks, we may underquote. If that risk becomes an issue, we may lose money on delivery and may have to abort the project.

Main purpose is to optimize the TCO profitability and not just the revenue.

Chapter 3.2.2. Co-relate Sales/Delivery/Operations and their Historic Data

To compute any TCO cost/profitability, we need to col-relate sales tasks to its delivery tasks - if a sale becomes a delivery, and/or operations tasks. Normally there's a substantial amount of overhead needed to check what we promised for a delivery and their accuracy may be subjective.

Typically, all individuals enter timesheets on a periodic basis using what's called a WBS Code. Main purpose of WBS code (with sub-codes) is to control financial figures for the effort. Normally WBS codes for Sales, Delivery, and Operations are quite independent.

Let's say the WBS Code for a sales project is WBS1 and we win the deal and the WBS code for the same delivery project (task) is WBS2, and it also needs operational services (like DBA/System Admin), and the WBS code for operations for same task is WBS3.

Let's change the WBS codes for sales project to WBS1-S, delivery project (task) to WBS1-D, and project operations to WBS1-O.

That will automatically link all of them and all data is auto-captured, and it's simple to analyze all TCO relationships as shown in the diagram below.

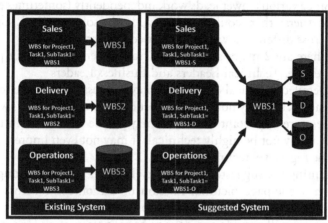

Fig 3.2.1 Co-relate WBS Codes across Lifecycle

Chapter 3.2.3. Impress Business/Technical Leaders of Potential Customers:

Especially during pre-sales, we may need to provide a response to a Request for Proposal (RFP), Request for Information (RFI), Request for Quote (RFQ), Request for Bid (RFB) etc. (generalized called RFX).

RFX provides what is customer's requirement and its response by us provides how we plan to provide the outcome.

Normally, companies provide great technical documents across different areas (also called Towers such as Data Engineering, Infrastructure, Project Management, Training, Testing, Enterprise Architecture etc.), each covering full details of what is required, how we plan to accomplish it, and why we are better than our competitors? So, they start with multiple technical leads from various towers right from the beginning while responding back to RFX regardless of the probability of bidding/winning.

There are three major problems with these responses i.e.

1. When we start with resources from various towers, we start with big overheads even though the probability/intent of winning the deal may be very low. We can know more details of whether we want to bid/or not, or whether we may win the deal over time. So why to assign too many resources to start with

2. Since various tower leads work independently (sometimes external partners), there could be a big gap in the solutions/tools suggested across different towers and their collaboration

3. There are 2 major stakeholders from potential customer point of view i.e. Technical Leaders and Business Leaders

4. Detailed technical documents may impress some of the technical leaders, but may not impress most of the business leaders who may be more important since they may decide who will win the deal but may not be highly technical. It may not even impress some of the high level technical leaders

We are naming the suggested solution as '**Pictorial Walk Through**' that starts with a one-page pictorial mission of the outcome across various towers, followed with some details of common portion. As we get more knowledge, we will provide one-page pictorial presentation for each tower followed with some details. It can be drilled down further (horizontally and/or vertically) as needed and finally full technical details.

Diagram below is a sample top level pictorial walk-through for a deal which is primarily data related.

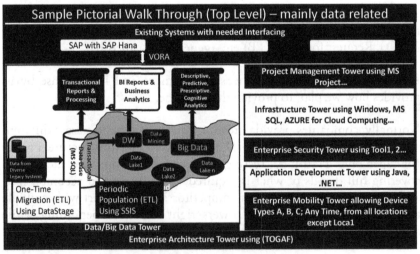

Fig 3.2.2 Pictorial Walk Through

This can solve all 3 problems shown above i.e.:

1. We can start with very few generic resources that provide high level pictorial presentations with some details (input from experts if needed). As we know more details/probability of bidding/winning, we can get more resources and provide more details
2. Moreover, it provides better collaboration across various towers
3. It can impress the potential customer (both business/technical leaders) and they can drill down the proposals to the extent, they like

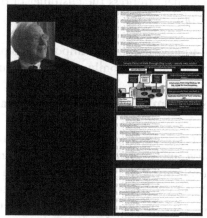

Fig 3.2.3 Pictorial Walk-Through Impresses Business Leaders

A picture may be worth huge number of words and can impress the business and technical leaders and they may like to get more details about that response.

Chapter 3.2.4. Minimize Sales/Pre-Sales expenses:

It's very important to minimize the cost of Marketing/Sales based upon the chances of winning the deal and the amount of overall TCO profitability.

Besides minimizing expenses using Pictorial Walk Through explained above, we may need additional steps shown below:

a. Reuse artifacts from previous response by creating document templates, tools to generate the documents
b. Templates/tools to provide quotes, assumptions, risks, gold-plating, dependencies, staffing, services, partnerships, hardware/software, real-estate, and other resources based upon historic patterns
c. Estimate the probability of winning the deals/TCO profitability based upon various historic factors, our competitors, who are main

decision makers and any issues with our relationships with those decision-makers, how serious is the customer (is this an RFI or RFP?), how much customer is willing to spend, do we have any realistic good/bad past relationship with the customer, and many other factors

Chapter 3.2.5. Proof of Concept (Prototyping)

It's important to confirm that our understanding of what the customer needs is correct. It can help impress the customer of our understanding, and high probability of delivering proper product.

Doesn't matter what tool we use, but it's important to provide a prototype as 'Proof of Concept' and if it's an online product, ensure its security.

Chapter 3.2.6. Go-to-market (GTM) i.e. What to Sell

- What to sell traditionally depends upon customer's needs/desires, our capability/supply, what our competitors can provide, and who are the incumbents with issues. As an example, what happens if we sell 220-volt electric products to USA (where normally 110-volt electric supply is available), or 110-volt products to another country where normally 220-volt supply is available.
- Besides winning the deal, more important is to have proper data to check TCO so that we can increase overall short/long-term profitability based on all tangible/ intangible factors.
- We also need to review our Strengths, Weaknesses, Opportunities, and Threats and convert Weaknesses into Strengths and Threats into Opportunities
- Look at factors across various domains i.e. political, social, economic, ethical, legal, technical, and mindset-paradigm shift factors. Easiest to simulate/resolve are technical factors and most difficult are mindsets i.e. if people are crazy about a brand due to whatever reason regardless of its quality/cost, how to sell other products besides controlling cost and quality?

Chapter 3.2.7. Market Dynamics i.e. how much to price?

How much should we charge for a product/service? Traditionally, it depends upon supply/demand besides various regulations. Price should depend upon various factors including historic data to maximize TCO profitability.

Chapter 3.2.8. POV (Point of View) i.e. How Real is what we recommend?

POV is related to Recommendations vs. Reality. This is where prescriptive analytics comes into the picture. Traditionally prescriptive analytics refers to suggestions vs. reality. But how do we know the accuracy of our prescription?

We would like to add important input to collect all our past predictive analytics and what actually happened and use those gaps as another important input as confidence level to our POV.

As an example, if we analyze Market Investment and predict what is our expected rate of return and risk in the next quarter, and based upon various activities going around the world, prescribe how accurate is our Predictive Analytics?

Another important way could be – Look at all the past quarters, analyze what would have been our prediction based upon the data prior to that quarter and what was the real results for that quarter. Use that as a base for prescriptive analytics to be more realistic.

Chapter 3.2.9. Negotiation:

There are 2 main ways to negotiate

1. **Win-Lose:** If we are going to have a short-term collaboration with a customer where we don't care about next-time sale, we should be able to make profit without caring whether the customer wins or loses.
2. **Win-Win:** If we want to maintain a good relationship with a customer and continue selling a product or other products, if the customer loses on that sale, he/she will not continue buying more products. Therefore, we should negotiate in a way that both parties win. This may be true for most of business (B2B) deals.

Sub-Section 3.3

Project Management

Chapter 3.3.1. Purpose of Project Management

A project manager is not the one who decides what product/service to deliver (decided by the leadership team).

Once what to deliver is decided with its requirements such as when to deliver, total cost, any governance rules etc., it's the responsibility of project management to deliver the expected outcome.

To accomplish the outcome, there are many areas required to achieve their goals such as:

- Technology
- Business
- Process
- Organization
- Information

Each of these areas can have further sub-areas like Technology may include Infrastructure, Applications, Enterprise Architecture, Security and more.

Based upon final outcome (Target Architecture or 'To-Be') and current status (Existing Architecture or 'As-Is'), each area/sub-area may need to delivered in multiple phases. Chapter 1.2.15 (Balance As-Is vs. To-Be scenario) shows an example of reaching moon where we might need to enhance the current launching speed to escape velocity (~25,000 miles/hour) in multiple phases.

The leaders of each area/sub-area will work to accomplish the outcome for each phase.

It's the responsibility of Project Management to co-ordinate various phases (or iterations) across various areas/sub-areas and accomplish the final outcome.

Projects are utilized as means of achieving an organization's strategic plan.

Project Management is a thread of people, processes, and technology in real-time -> to achieve optimal business value

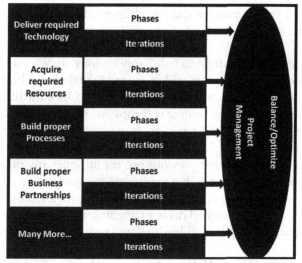

Fig 3.3 Project Management

There are 3 major task categories needed for project management i.e.

- **Collaboration:** A project manager needs to collaborate across all areas/ sub-areas to optimize their compatibility and provide best project plans to accomplish the outcome
- **Visibility:** Need to find real-time status of various needs. Here are some examples:
  - ➢ A person is suddenly not available
  - ➢ There is an earth-quake at a particular location
  - ➢ Some hardware has stopped working
  - ➢ Some useful data has been corrupted
  - ➢ A new governance rule has arrived
  - ➢ A task has taken more/less time than planned
  - ➢ A risk has become an issue
  - ➢ A partner has gone out of business
  - ➢ A particular task cost was more/less than planned
  - ➢ ...
- **Dynamic Re-distribution:** Although the project plan was provided based upon various initial parameters, real-time visibility of data has to be taken as input to dynamically re-distribute various actions and resources

Project vs. Operations: A project is a temporary endeavor to build a unique product/service whereas Operations are repetitive and ongoing.

Let's say we need to provide daily backup of all data for a customer, it needs 2 main parts:

1. To create all infrastructure, applications, tools, and testing to build the product that will be able to take daily backups. This is a project that will create a unique product. Once the infrastructure is completed – the project is completed i.e. it's temporary. If after some time, plans change to backup with different requirements or technology changes, we may need to create the new project which is different from the previous project (unique) and once that new project is over, again that's complete (temporary).
2. Once that product is ready, we need to provide daily services to provide the backups. This is an ongoing and repetitive process that is repeated regularly. This is related to service/operations.

Chapter 3.3.2. Water Fall vs. Iterative/Agile Methodologies

Let's say, we plan to have a dinner party for which we have to prepare various dinner recipes. Shown below are 2 ways to implement this:

1. Decide all recipes, then buy all grocery items needed to prepare those recipes, then cut all vegetables, then cook all recipes, then test all recipes, and finally set the party
2. Decide some recipes, buy grocery items for those recipes, while cutting vegetables for those recipes – add more recipes and buy more grocery items and cut more vegetables, cook some recipes, test them and cook some more recipes and test them, set the party and add more recipes as needed. In other words, while working on any step, may need to go back to previous steps.

Let's say the salt we are using is too spicy. In the first situation, all recipes will be spicy since we will test them after all are prepared.

In the second situation, when we test the first set of recipes, we will learn that the salt is more spicy and we can adjust it properly while cooking next recipes.

First example is similar to what's called 'Water Fall methodology' where all the actions are divided into various phases and phase n+1 starts after phase n is completed and once a phase starts and its prior phase is complete, you can't go back to previous phases. Only overlap could be – when you initiate phase n+1, you may still be completing phase n.

Second example is similar to 'Iterative methodology' (aka 'Agile methodology'), where various actions (phases, iterations) are going in parallel i.e. one phase may have multiple iterations and if action1 is going through phase1, action2 may be going through phase2 at the same time and so on.

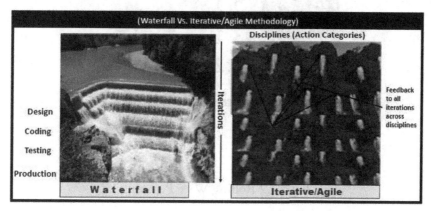

Fig 3.3.1 Waterfall versus Iterative/Agile Methodology

Both methodologies have their pros/cons such as:

If we know the plan very well and the variations are very less, waterfall methodology is less expensive, whereas if there are many variations (like salt too spicy), it's easy to adjust changes in Iterative/Agile methodology.

Chapter 3.3.3. Water Fall Project Management

One of the well-known waterfall methodology is provided by Project Management Institute (PMI) that provides various certifications including PMP (Project Management Professional), PgMP (Program Management Professional), CAPM (Certified Associate in Project Management - managed by a guide called Project Management Body of Knowledge (PMBOK). Other famous tools are PRINCE2, Mevenlink and many more.

This chapter provides some major terms of the PMI waterfall methodology, mainly PMBOK versions 5.

Progressive Elaboration (Rolling Wave Planning) approach:

When you are applying water to your garden using the water hose with a water hose reel, you keep the hose in the reel until you get closer to the place where you have to unroll it due to the distance, same goes for a project.

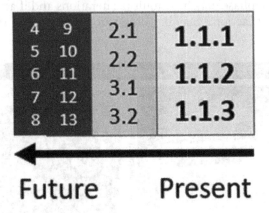

Fig 3.3.2 Rolling Wave Planning

You provide high level summary for all future activities and drill-down to details as time comes closer to the activity. That's called Rolling Wave Planning or Progressive Elaboration where activities are developed in steps and continued by increments.

Triple Constraints:

There are various aspects (constraints) that may impact each other and for best results, they may need to be balanced. Three major constraints are:

- **Cost:** If due to various reasons, cost of the project goes up, what can be done to reduce the cost? Can we delay project completion? Can we reduce some of the requirements (scope) that were agreed - to reduce the cost?
- **Time:** If the project gets delayed, can we supplement resources that will add to the cost? Can we reduce some of the committed requirements (scope)?
- **Scope:** What is the scope of user/business requirements? If we couldn't complete all the requirements, can we delay the project or increase the project cost?

Although these are typically considered as triple constraints, some other constraints may also be co-related such as 'Quality' and 'Risk'. In other words, we can make quality better or reduce the risk with impact on other constraints.

Project Hierarchy: Program, Project, Subproject; Project Management Office (PMO), Project Portfolio Management (PPM):

Let's say you want to consolidate a few data centers to a single consolidated data center.

This might need multiple areas such as building of real estate, consolidation of all hardware infrastructure, applications, resources, service help desk, and many more.

Each one of these may be considered as a **Project** and Project Managers can be assigned accordingly.

All these projects are related with a common mission, the overall data center consolidation may be considered as a **Program** with a **Program Manager** assigned.

If a portion of the project is outsourced, it's difficult to manage that portion of the project at the sub level by the Project Manager and that may be considered as a **Sub-Project**.

There might be some standard practices, processes, templates, available resources... within the business for different major areas like

- Infrastructure management
- Applications Development
- Outsourcing
- etc.

These are examples of various **Project Management Offices (PMO)**, which are groups within the business to define/maintain standards for projects within that group. In other words, all programs and projects within a PMO belong to similar categories although those projects/programs are different. Purpose of PMO is to define common templates, guidelines, resources, etc. for all projects/programs within that PMO.

How do we ensure that all projects, programs, PMO relationships are properly synchronized and there are common processes, techniques, analysis, and resources to track, monitor, and improve activities to achieve overall profitability across all projects? That is managed by **Project Portfolio Management** (PPM) and includes various areas so called **Portfolios**. This entire book for 'Strategic Balancing' is related to PPM.

Project Lifecycle:

As explained in chapter 3.3.2 (Water Fall vs. Iterative/Agile Methodologies) above on comparison between Waterfall and Iterative methodology, waterfall projects are typically completed in phases where phases are completed in sequence i.e. you start phase1, then phase2 and so on although there could be some overlap i.e. you may start phase2 while phase1 is still being completed. However, you can't go back to phase1 after phase1 is completed.

The entire set of phases is called as the **Project Lifecycle.**

Fig 3.3.3 Waterfall Methodology

Sponsor:

The individual who authorizes a project

Stakeholders:

All individuals who are part of the project, who may impact the project outcome, or who may be impacted by the project outcome are stakeholders and may include:

- Project/Program Manager and Management teams
- Project/Program Team Members
- Customers and Users across lines of business/domains
- Sponsor
- PMO
- ...

Gold Plating:

If we need to provide certain features as part of project requirements, but we try to add other feature(s) not committed per agreement but to attract the customer, that is called **Gold Plating**.

Whether it's worth/not depends upon various factors such as amount of extra expense, what's the potential benefit in the long run, and more importantly any additional risk added by unnecessary feature.

Let's say you buy a car - and you get free car mats, or free initial – it may not be bad. Even getting free coffee/drinks/snacks at a luxury car seller may not be bad.

If for a patient, you provide a free medicine and that may have some side effects, that can be extremely risky.

Communication Channels:

How many one to one interfaces do we need for communications? If there are 'N' persons, each person may talk to 'N-1' individuals but that includes both sides, so for N persons, total communication channels would be $N*(N-1)/2$

Estimated Monetary Value (EMV):

If there are multiple options, how do you compare those options to find which one has the best profitability. EMV is one way where you find various activities for each option with their probability to compare them.

Let's take an example of buying a TV model1.

I have 2 options i.e. buy from a store for $2,000, or let's say the same TV is coming on sale tomorrow on 'Thanksgiving Black Friday' at a particular store for $1,500.

Which is better option?

For option1, there's hardly any time/travel involved and there's ~100% guarantee of buying TV.

So, the total cost for Option 1 is 100% of $2,000 = $2.000

For option 2, one may need to spend many hours (that too early morning outside in real winter time), plus the distance may be large. Let's say the additional cost of travel/time/botheration is $300.

Let's say there's only 50% probability that one may be able to get the TV on sale. If not, one will need to buy at regular price i.e.

So, the total cost for Option 2 is

$300 + 50%*$1,500 + 50% of $2,000 i.e. $300+$750+$1,000 = $2,050

Work Breakdown Structure (WBS):

Work Breakdown Structure is a method to decompose various tasks to proper executable level. The purpose is to decompose/drill-down at a level (called **Work Package**) where the cost can be estimated, it can be scheduled, monitored, and controlled. Work package can be sub-divided into activities and it is used as a base for total cost.

Total cost is computed as:

- Add cost of various Activities to get cost of Work Package
- Add cost of work packages to get the cost per **Control Account** (across different accounts under general ledger)
- Add cost of control accounts to get **cost of the project**
- Then add the cost related to coverage of various risks (like paying for medical insurance, spares for backup etc.) called **Contingency Reserve** to get the **Cost Baseline**

- Then add the cost of additional management reservation for safety (called **Management Reserve**) to finally compute the **Cost Budget**.

Activity Dependency:

There are mainly 4 types of dependencies between two Activities (Act1, and Act2) i.e.:

1. Act2 can't start until Act1 is completed
2. Act2 can't be completed until Act1 is complete
3. Act2 can't start until Act1 is started
4. Act2 can't be completed until Act1 is started

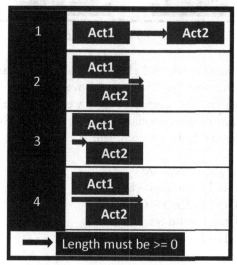

Fig 3.3.4 Activity Dependency

The dependency can be forced (**Mandatory**) like you can't start second floor until first floor base is completed; or **Discretionary** where it's not forced but desired, like complete the master bed room first and then the other rooms on the same floor due to certain desired logic.

Another two important terms are called **Lead** and **Lag**. In a Lead, the Act2 can start before Act1 is finished whereas in Lag there has to be Lag after Act1 is finished and then Act2 starts.

An example of Lead can be Software Design and Development, where Development can start while Design is still being completed; whereas if we are starting second level, we have to finish Floor11, and then may have to wait before that gets completed & dried and then start Floor2.

Critical Path:

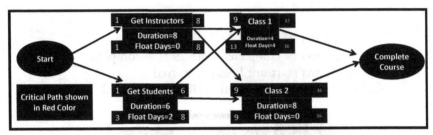

Fig 3.3.5 Critical Path

Let's take a situation where 2 classes (Class1 and Class2) are required to complete a course (shown in the above diagram). We need to get the instructors and the students before we can start either of the two classes. Let's assume that no class can start until both 'Get Instructors' and 'Get Students' tasks are complete.

The durations for 4 tasks are:
1. Get Instructors – 8 days
2. Get Students – 6 days
3. Class1 – 4 days
4. Class2 – 8 days

There are 2 set of total activities going in parallel i.e.:

Class1 = (Get Instructors/Get Students) => (Class1) i.e. Max (8, 6) + 4 = 12 Days
Class2 = (Get Instructors/Get Students) => (Class2) i.e. Max (8, 6) + 8 = 16 Days

***Critical Path** is the longest time of various parallel activities i.e. 16 days for the project. If we started the project on Jan 1st, it will finish on Jan 16th (assuming all days as working days).*

Another important factor is called float days that includes 'Early Start', 'Early Finish', 'Late Start', 'Late Finish', 'Float Days' for each task and 'Total Float Days' for each parallel activity.

'Early Start': Earliest a task can start without impacting the project completion date.
'Late Start': Latest a task can start without impacting the project completion date.
'Early Finish': Earliest a task can finish without impacting the project completion date.
'Late Finish': Latest a task can finish without impacting the project completion date.
'Float Days': Total Extra days for each task.
'Total Float Days': Total Extra days for each parallel activity.

For all tasks of the critical path, the 'Early Start' = 'Late Start' and 'Early Finish' = 'Late Finish'. Moreover, 'Float Days' for each task of critical path and 'Total Float Days' for the critical path are all zero.

In the diagram above, 'Early Start' for each task is shown on top left, 'Late Start' of bottom left, 'Early Finish' on top right, and 'Late Finish' on bottom right.

'Early Start' depends upon the latest finish date for the previous tasks that are dependent on this and latest finish date depends upon the earliest date the next dependent tasks can start. 'Early Finish' can be computed based upon 'Early Start' and 'Late Start' can be computed based upon 'Late Finish'.

Since 'Get Instructors' doesn't depend upon any previous task, it's 'Early Start' is day1, and thus 'Early Finish' is day 6.

However, 'Get Instructors' finishing depends upon starting of class2 which starts on day 9, its 'Late Finish' is 8 and thus 'Late Start' is 3.

Class1 staring depends upon finishing of 'Get Instructors' and can't start before day 9. Since it's duration is 4 days, its 'Early Start' is 9 and 'Early Finish' is 12.

Class1 must be completed by day 16 and so it's 'Late Finish' is 16, and thus 'Early Finish' is 13.

The 'Float Days' for a task can be computed by the number of days between 'Late Finish' and 'Early Start' minus duration i.e. for 'Get Students' it's 8 - 6 = 2 days and for 'Class1', it's 8 – 4 = 4 days.

'Total Float Days' for Activity 1 i.e.
(Get Instructors/Get Students) => (Class1) is 2 +4 = 6 days.

Organizational Structure:

An organization can be structured in 3 major categories i.e.:

Functional:

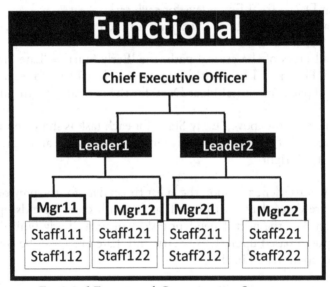

Fig 3.3.6 Functional Organization Structure

Managers and Leaders are responsible for various functions such as Leader1 is responsible for Sales, and Leader2 for Delivery; Mgr11 responsible for Sales in Telecom industry and so on. Each manager has staff directly reporting to the manager and is working as a People Manager.

When a project starts, staff from various functions are assigned to that project (say Staff112, Staff211, and Staff222) working on a project.

Projectized:

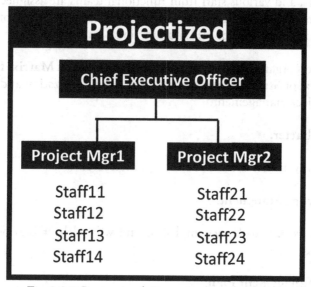

Fig 3.3.7 Projectized Organization Structure

Employees are hired/assigned based on projects only and report to the Project Manager.

Matrix:

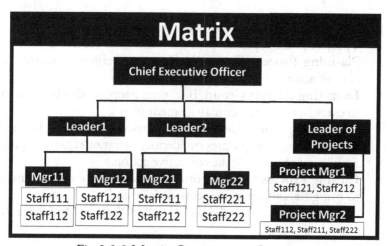

Fig 3.3.8 Matrix Organization Structure

Matrix organization is a combination of Functional and Projectized Organization. Staff reports to the Functional Managers. There's another

Project Management team and Project Managers are assigned to various projects, and various staff from functional teams are assigned to those projects. The staff reports to both i.e. Project Manager for the project and functional manager for HR and functional purpose as people manager.

A matrix organization could be considered as **Weak Matrix**, **Balanced Matrix**, or **Strong Matrix** based upon the authorization and strength of project management.

Project Charter:

Formally authorizes the project at a high level.

Project Scope Statement:

What work is to be accomplished and what deliverables need to be produced.

Project Management Plan:

How the work will be performed. Project Management System is a set of tools, techniques, methodologies, resources, and procedures to manage a project.

Process Groups:

- **Initiating Process Group**. Defines and authorizes the project or a project phase typically with the creation of Project Charter
- **Planning Process Group**. Defines and refines objectives, and plan of action to attain the project objectives
- **Executing Process Group**. Integrates people and other resources to carry out the project management plan
- **Monitoring and Controlling Process Group**. Regularly measures/monitors progress to identify variations from the project management plan to take corrective action
- **Closing Process Group**. Formalizes acceptance of the outcome to bring the project/phase to an orderly end
  Another similar approach is Deming PDCA (Plan-Do-Check-Act).

Process:

Set of inter-related actions performed to achieve pre-defined output performed by the project team.

Project team selects process sub-sets from the Project Management Process Groups that are required to meet the project objectives.

Standard processes can be customized as needed which is called **Tailoring.**

Risk:

Uncertain event that may have positive or negative effect on part of the project objective. If the risk becomes a positive or negative effect, that's called an **Issue.**

Negative Risks are called **Threats** and positive risks are called **Opportunities.** Two of the main factors of Risk are Probability and Impact for both Threats and Opportunities. **Probability** defines the probability of a risk becoming an issue whereas **Impact** is the worth (negative or positive) of the issue.

There are 3 common ways to deal with a threat i.e.

- **Avoid:** Ignore it
- **Transfer:** Transfer the risk to a third-party like outsourcing for software development
- **Mitigate:** An approach to reduce the impact and/or probability of the risk becoming an issue. Examples of mitigation could be to buy medical insurance, fault tolerance to duplicate hardware/data

There are 3 common ways to deal with an opportunity i.e.:

- **Share:** Share the opportunity where all are ready to pay for the risk and share the profits - like partnerships
- **Enhance:** Increase the probability of risk becoming an opportunity (not guaranteed). The earlier you bid for a special sale, the higher the probability of getting that special deal
- **Exploit:** Ensure 100% probability of risk becoming an opportunity (not guaranteed). An example could be, if you pay an initial fee (like 529 plan in USA), you will get free tuition for your kids

There are 2 common ways to deal with a threat or opportunity i.e.:

- **Contingent Response Strategy (or Wait):** Sometimes, a pre-event may happen before there's high probability of a risk becoming an issue. In that case, you may wait to take an action till that event happens. This process is called **Contingent Response Strategy.** An example could be to buy the Earth Quake insurance after a news comes showing high probability of earth quake in that area

- **Accept:** If not much can be done before hand, or the impact is low, one can accept the risk when it becomes an issue without any extra protection expense beforehand.

Schedule Compression:

There could be various techniques to follow - if it appears that an activity will be delayed i.e. taking care of schedule compression. We believe, here are the best steps in order where you can take steps with minimum side effects first i.e.:

1. Confirm the calculations are correct for showing the delay
2. Check for gold plating and the assumptions i.e. are we providing an activity not required by the customer that's causing delay, or some of the assumptions are not correct?
3. Confirm Dependencies and try to do activities in parallel (aka Fast Tracking). If we thought activity2 can't start unless activity1 is finished but that was not correct, can they can start in parallel?
4. Reshuffle Resources (aka Crashing). If two parallel activities are taking 4 and 8 hours but we have less efficient (or count) of resources for the activity taking 8 hours - if we reshuffle the resources, they might take 6 hours (or lesser) for each
5. Last step would be - talk to the customer and see if we can impact some other constraint to reduce the time constraint i.e. reduce scope, increase cost, reduce quality

Earned Value Techniques:

These are the calculations to check the performance of cost/schedule.

Let's say we are planning to build 5 rooms, each room worth $1,000, and expected completion time for each room is 1 day.

However, at the end of Day3:
We have built 2.5 rooms
We have spent $2,300

Are we **Behind/Ahead** of **Schedule** – How much?
Have we **Overspent/Underspent** – How much?

It's computed based upon 3 parameters i.e. PV (Planned Value) i.e. what should have been accomplished, EV (Earned Value) i.e. what has been accomplished, and AC (Actual Cost).

At the end of Day3:
    Planned Value (PV): 3.0 * $1,000 = $3,000
    Earned Value (EV): 2.5 * $1,000 = $2,500
    Actual Cost (AC): = $2,300

Here are main calculations:

Schedule Variance (SV): EV – PV = $2,500 – $3,000 = -$500
    (<0 means behind schedule, 0 means on schedule, >0 means Ahead of schedule)

Schedule Performance Index (SPI) = EV/PV = 2500/3000 = .8333
    (<1 means behind schedule, 1 means on schedule, >1 means Ahead of schedule)

Cost Variance (CV): EV – AC = $2,500 – $2,300 = +$200
    (<0 means overspent, 0 means on spent as expected, >0 means underspent)

Cost Performance Index (SPI) = EV/AC = 2500/2300 = 1.087
    (<1 means overspent, 1 means on spent as expected, >1 means underspent)

So, we are behind schedule but underspent.

Roles and Responsibility, i.e. Responsibility Assignment Matrix or (RACI):

- **R (Responsible):** Responsible to achieve a task. One or more
- **A (Accountable):** Overall accountable. Just one person
- **C (Consultant):** Who are consulted for their opinion with response/activities
- **I (Informed):** Who need to be informed – just one-way communication

There can be 2 more roles/responsibilities i.e. -VS (or RACI-VS):

- **V (Verifier):** Who verifies and accepts the product
- **S (Signatory):** Who approves the verification and authorizes the product. Typically, same person who's A (accountable)

Knowledge Areas:

There are various knowledge areas with many processes and each process has Input, Output, Tools and Techniques i.e. Project Management Processes and Product-Oriented Processes.

Although all knowledge areas have their own details, here are general type of inputs, and Tools/Techniques used for most of knowledge areas:

Typical Process Inputs
- Contract
- Project Charter
- Project Statement of Work
- Enterprise Environmental Factors
- Organizational Process Assets
- Scope Statement
- Change Requests
- Corrective Actions
- Activity List
- Resource Availability
- Work Breakdown Structure

Typical Process Tools/Techniques:
- Expert Judgment
- Project Management Information System
- Project Management Methodology
- Project Selection Method
- Earned Value Technique
- Decomposition
- Alternatives Analysis
- Bottom-up Estimating
- Published Estimating Data
- Analogous Estimating
- Parametric Estimating
- Three-Point Estimates (Most likely, Optimistic, Pessimistic)

Knowledge Areas: (Project Management Grouped by Specialties)

Here is a summary of various knowledge areas:

- **Integration Management:** Effectively integrating all processes across knowledge areas required to accomplish the project objectives within an organization's defined procedures
- **Scope Management:** Project Scope Management includes the processes required to ensure that the project includes all commitments, and only the work required, to complete the project successfully
- **Time Management:** Ensures timely completion of the project
- **Cost Management:** Includes the processes involved in planning, estimating, budgeting, and controlling costs so that the project can be completed within the approved budget
- **Quality Management:** Project Quality Management processes include all the activities of the performing organization that determine quality policies, objectives, and responsibilities so that the project will satisfy the needs for which it was undertaken
- **HR Management:** Project Human Resource Management includes the processes that organize and manage the project team
- **Communications Management:** Proper communication of timely and appropriate generation, collection, distribution, storage, retrieval, and ultimate disposition of project information – between all related stakeholders
- **Risk Management:** Concerned with conducting risk management planning, identification, analysis, response, and monitoring/control on a project throughout the project. Its objective is to increase the probability/impact of positive events, and decrease the probability/impact of negative events
- **Procurement Management:** Includes the processes to purchase or acquire the products, services, or results needed from outside the project team to perform the work
- **Stakeholder Management:** Develop proper management strategy to optimize stakeholders throughout the project lifecycle, based on various requirements and practical approach Each knowledge area has some processes that will be used under different process groups. Shown below is a high definition of each knowledge area followed by processes across different process groups:

Knowledge Area	Processes across Process Groups				
	Initiation	Planning	Execution	Monitoring & Control	Closing
1 Integration Management	• Develop Project Charter	• Develop Project Management Plan	• Direct & Manage Work	• Monitor & Control Project Work • Perform Integrated Change Control	• Close Project or Phase
2 Scope Management		• Plan Scope • Collect Requirements • Define Scope • Create WBS		• Verify Scope • Control Scope	
3 Time Management		• Plan Schedule Management • Define Activities • Sequence Activities • Estimate Activity Resources • Estimate Activity Duration • Develop Schedule		• Control Schedule	
4 Cost Management		• Plan Cost • Estimate Costs • Determine Budget		• Control Costs	
5 Quality Management		• Plan Quality Management	• Perform Quality Assurance	• Perform Quality Control	
6 HR Management		• Plan HR Management	• Acquire Project Team • Develop Project Team • Manage Project Team		
7 Communications Management		• Plan Communications Management	• Manage Communications	• Control Communications	
8 Risk Management		• Plan Risk • Identify Risks • Perform Qualitative Risk Analysis • Perform Quantitative Risk Analysis • Plan Risk Response		• Control Risks	
9 Procurement Management		• Plan Procurements Management	• Conduct Procurements	• Control Procurements	• Close Procurements
10 Stakeholder Management	• Identify Stakeholders	• Plan Stakeholder Management	• Manage Stakeholder Engagement	• Control Stakeholder Engagement	• Get Stakeholder feedback

Chapter 3.3.4. Iterative/Agile Project Management

In waterfall methodology, various phases for all areas/disciplines are done one after the other, but not exactly like that in iterative/agile methodology.

As an example, if we are constructing a multi-story building, floor n+1 starts only after floor n base is completed under waterfall methodology.

Shown below is an example where the outside base of three sections was completed first and then the three sections (Activities – each containing multiple floors) were built in parallel. It's kind of an agile/iterative process where multiple phases are being delivered in parallel and each phase has multiple iterations.

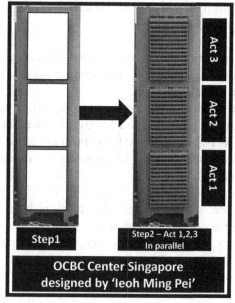

Fig 3.3.9 OCBC Center Singapore

There are many methodologies related to agile/iterative processing. We are going to cover mainly Scrum, and RUP (Rational Unified Process) with UML (Unified Modeling Language).

Chapter 3.3.5. Scrum

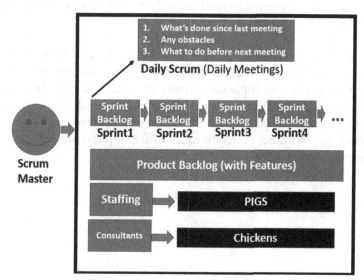

Fig 3.3.10 Scrum Methodology

Here are main highlights of Scrum which is an Agile framework to implement all kind of projects

- All requirements that may be implemented and dynamically changed over time based upon customer/business desires are listed in **Product Backlog**
- A sub-set of those requirements is decided as part of planning before starting each iteration (usually 2-4 weeks) which is called **Sprint**. The features selected for a Sprint are called **Sprint Backlog**
- Within each sprint, each business day, a meeting is arranged (**Daily Scrum**)
- Each Daily Scrum meeting is pretty small (~15 minutes) to check – what is done, any issues, and what needs to be done next
- Any features not implemented in a sprint, are re-analyzed before starting next sprint i.e. whether they should be part of next sprint backlog, product backlog, or removed
- Overall in-charge is called **Scrum Master**
- An internal staff member is called **Pig** and an external member is called **Chicken**. One logic for these terms being – as internal candidates we are eating the entire pig, for external candidates, we are just eating the egg of the chicken – still keeping the chicken alive

Chapter 3.3.6. Rational Unified Process (RUP)

The Rational Unified Process (RUP) is an iterative software development process framework created by the Rational Software Corporation, and later bought by IBM since 2003.

In Waterfall methodology, a project is divided in phases; whereas in Scrum, a project is divided in Iterations. RUP is a good combination of both where a project has multiple disciplines, and each discipline has multiple phases, and each phase has multiple iterations – where different disciplines work in parallel (although some activities can't be in parallel based upon dependencies). Number of iterations for different phases/disciplines can be different as shown below:

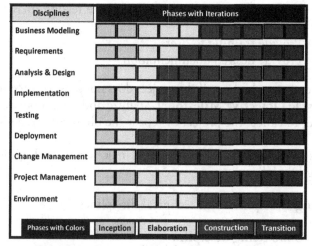

Disciplines	Phases with Iterations
Business Modeling	
Requirements	
Analysis & Design	
Implementation	
Testing	
Deployment	
Change Management	
Project Management	
Environment	
Phases with Colors	Inception	Elaboration	Construction	Transition

Fig 3.3.11 Rational Unified Process (RUP)

Here are highlights of the 4 main phases:

Inception phase
- Get Requirements and define Scope
- Plan cost/benefit analysis

Elaboration phase
- Define the basic architecture and description of software architecture
- Analyze the basic problems
- Complete the major use-case models to good extent
- Explore risk list and analyze their impacts/probability
- Development plan for the overall project
- Develop prototypes (proof of concept) where needed and collaborate with stakeholders for any changes

Construction phase
- Develop actual systems with all activities
- Complete testing of individual components (unit testing), followed by functional, system integration, and regression testing
- Release the first external phase of the software and collaborate with end user stake-holders to get feedback iteratively

Transition phase
- Transition the product from the development environment to user environment

- Perform Beta testing and Acceptance testing (may be by the customer)
- Provide training to users
- Provide desired documentation

At the end of each phase, if the project does not pass required milestone (**Lifecycle Objective Milestone**), analyze and take proper action i.e. whether to cancel the project or repeat the phase after redesign.

Highlights of 9 main disciplines across 2 major areas i.e. Engineering & Supporting Disciplines:

Engineering Disciplines: All technical disciplines

Business modeling discipline
- Describes the vision and mission based upon business/customer requirements, market trend, business capabilities and other factors.
- This will be used as the base for deployment

Requirements discipline
- Convert external requirements into internal system requirements i.e. take what's required by the business/customer as input and convert that into detailed requirements (mostly technical) as to what the system must do to accomplish them

Analysis and design discipline
- Analyze the system requirements and find the best way to implement them
- Build technical architecture
- Build design model and use-case descriptions, plus prototypes if needed

Implementation discipline
- Implement to system components with their internal testing (unit testing)
- Ensure proper interface across components

Test discipline
- Test interaction between system components
- Perform Beta testing in a production environment
- Co-ordinate with the customer/users for acceptance testing

- Since RUP is highly iterative process, learn issues from each iteration and fix it in next iteration

Deployment discipline
- Deliver the software to end users
- Provide any documentation/training as needed
- Maintain version/release controls

Supporting Disciplines: Business-related and other disciplines to support the technical disciplines

Configuration and Change management discipline
- Configure relationships for all assets and artifacts needed for the system
- Track/monitor all changes needed
- Maintain configuration system to adjust them based upon all changes
- Go through all necessary approvals for any changes to implement
- Keep audit of all change logs

Project management discipline - Phases, Iterations, and Work Products (Artifacts)
- Each phase within each discipline is treated like a project
- Based upon its complexity, divide the project in appropriate iterations
- Plan the project/iterations, co-ordinate across various resources, optimize the results based upon the availability of resources
- Track/monitor and adjust plans based upon real factors
- Adjust any changes
- Consolidate with various stakeholders as needed
- Maintain auditing of experience to serve as a learning in the future

Environment discipline
- Understand and plan the environment needs including tools, processes, infrastructure, buildings, travel needs, operational help, approvals, financial requirements
- Make adjustments as needed

Best Practices of RUP: Here are 6 main practices used within RUP

Develop iteratively
- Divide each phase within each discipline into appropriate iterations as needed

Manage requirements
- Managed by various stakeholders/entire team under control of the product owner

Use component architecture
- The architecture is outlined based upon full collaboration across the company's strategy, guidelines, technology, and requirements

Model visually
- RUP promotes visual modeling explained in chapter 3.3.7 'The Unified Modeling Language (UML)'

Continuously ensuring quality
- Learn from each iteration and improve their quality and learn across phases/disciplines

Manage change
- In Waterfall, changes are difficult to adjust once the project starts, in RUP it's much easier to allow/manage any adjustments/changes

Chapter 3.3.7. The Unified Modeling Language (UML)

Each industry has a standardized (sometimes visual) language to minimize communication gaps and maximize synchronization – Why not the Software Industry?

As an example, a blue print for the construction industry provides a good view of a real estate.

Moreover. orchestras are led by a conductor who directs the performance with movements of the hands and arms, using conductor's baton.

Unified Modeling Language (UML) is developed as a graphical language for visualizing, specifying, constructing, and documenting the artifacts of a software-intensive system. The Unified Modeling Language offers a standard way to write a system's blueprint, including conceptual items such as business processes and system functions as well as concrete items such as programming language statements, database schemas, and reusable software components.

UML has many different type of diagrams, some of these are highlighted below:

- **Use Case** diagrams are used to model user/system interactions. They define behavior, requirements and constraints in the form of scripts or scenarios

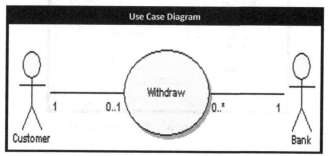

Fig 3.3.12 Use Case Diagram

- **Activity** diagrams have a wide number of uses, from defining basic program flow to capturing decision points and actions within any generalized process

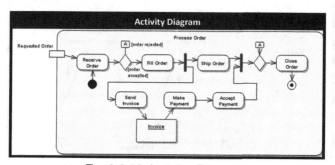

Fig 3.3.13 Activity Diagram

- **State Machine** diagrams are essential to understand the instant to instant condition, or "run state" of a model when it executes

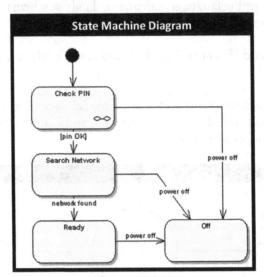

Fig 3.3.14 State Machine Diagram

- **Communication/Collaboration** diagrams show the network and sequence of messages or communications between objects at run-time, or during a collaboration instance

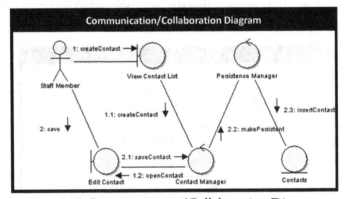

Fig 3.3.15 Communication/Collaboration Diagram

- **Sequence** diagrams are closely related to communication diagrams and show the sequence of messages passed between objects using a vertical timeline

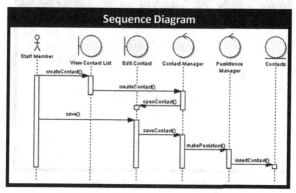

Fig 3.3.16 Sequence Diagram

- **Class/Structural** diagrams define the basic building blocks of a model: the types, classes and general materials used to construct a full model

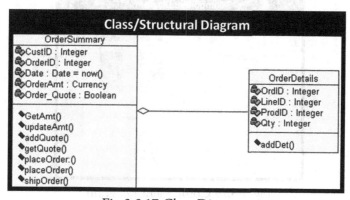

Fig 3.3.17 Class Diagram

- **Object** diagrams show how instances of structural elements are related and used at run-time

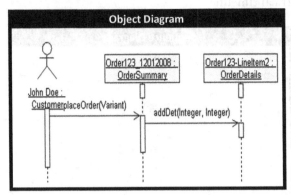

Fig 3.3.18 Object Diagram

- **Component** diagrams are used to model higher level or more complex structures, usually built up from one or more classes, and providing a well-defined interface

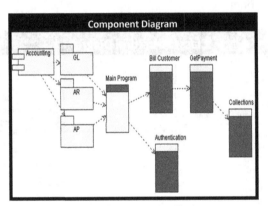

Fig 3.3.19 Component Diagram

- **Deployment** diagrams show the physical disposition of significant artifacts within a real-world setting

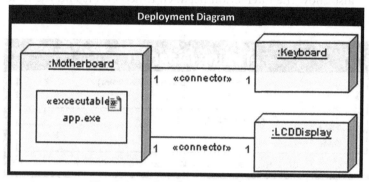

Fig 3.3.20 Deployment Diagram

- **Package** diagrams are used to reflect the organization of packages and their elements. When used to represent class elements, package diagrams provide a visualization of the namespaces. The most common use for package diagrams is to organize use case diagrams and class diagrams, although the use of package diagrams is not limited to these UML elements. Elements contained in a package share the same namespace. Therefore, the elements contained in a specific namespace must have unique names

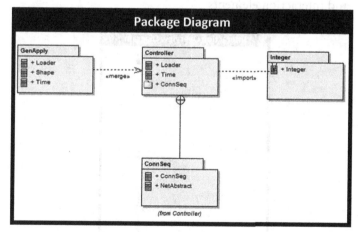

Fig 3.3.21 Package Diagram

- **Timing** Diagrams UML timing diagrams are used to display the change in state or value of one or more elements over time. It can also show the interaction between timed events and the time and duration constraints that govern them

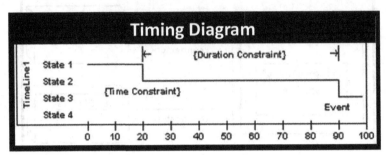

Fig 3.3.22 Timing Diagram

- **Interaction Overview** Diagrams An interaction overview diagram is a form of activity diagram in which the nodes represent interaction diagrams. Interaction diagrams can include sequence, communication, interaction overview and timing diagrams. Most of the notations for interaction overview diagrams are the same for activity diagrams. For example, initial, final, decision, merge, fork, and join nodes are all the same. However, interaction overview diagrams introduce two new elements: interaction occurrences and interaction elements

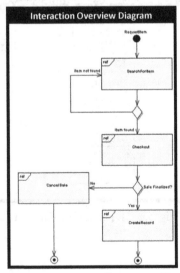

Fig 3.3.23 Interaction Overview Diagram

- **Composite structure** diagram is a diagram that shows the internal structure of a classifier, including its interaction points to other parts of the system. It shows the configuration and relationship of parts, that together perform the behavior of the containing classifier

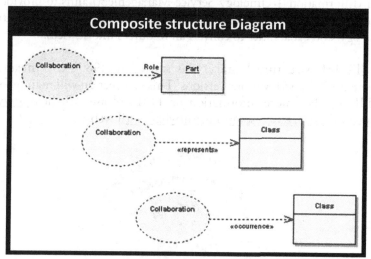

Fig 3.3.24 Composite Structure Diagram

Sub-Section 3.4

IT Service Management

ITSM (Information Technology Service Management) aims to provide IT services offered to customers based upon their policies, processes, organization, technology, and capabilities to convert all resources into services.

ITIL (IT Infrastructure Library) was started in 1980's as a means to implement ITSM with various versions. This sub-section will mainly focus on ITIL V3. For more information on ITIL, please visit https://www.axelos.com/best-practice-solutions/itil/what-is-itil website.

Fig 3.4 Service Management
(Hub and Spoke ITIL v3)

What's a Service?

Let's talk about many services for a house/car like:
- Lawn mowing, Furnace Cleaning, Painting, Sprinkler System Maintenance, Car Oil Change, Tire Change, More Complex Services etc.

There could be plenty of IT services to maintain all hardware, applications, backups ...

All these require some resources (like infrastructure, people, applications, financial capital, information ...) and their maintenance besides regular services. They involve some risk if performing improper services. Plus, other constraints.

A service is delivering value to customer by facilitating the desired outcomes without ownership of specific costs and risks. A service facilitates desired outcomes by enhancing performance and by reducing the influence of constraints.

What's Service management?

Anyone with proper funds can buy necessary resources. But you need special capabilities to transfer these resources into desired services.

Service Management is the art of transforming resources into valuable services by exploiting the organization's capabilities and that too with minimum total cost of ownership (TCO).

Chapter 3.4.1. Purpose of ITIL:

ITIL V2 was focused more of providing services based upon technology whereas V3 is focused more on customer/business needs. ITIL V3 has mainly 3 purposes:
1. Ensure that IT services are aligned based upon current/future requirements/needs/desires of business and customers
2. Improve quality of IT services delivered by continual service improvements
3. Optimize the cost by minimizing the Total Cost of Ownership (TCO) i.e. total lifecycle cost of the services

ITIL V3 contains mainly 2 streams i.e. **Lifecycle Stream** and **Capability Stream**.

Capability Stream contains four clusters i.e.
1. Operational Support and Analysis (OSA)
2. Service, Offerings, and Agreements (SOA)
3. Planning, Protection, and Optimization (PPO)
4. Release, Control, and Validation (RCV)

Lifecycle Stream contains 5 major services:
1. Service Strategy

2. Service Design
3. Service Transition
4. Service Operation
5. Continual Service Improvement.

We will focus of Lifecycle Stream

Chapter 3.4.2. Important ITIL Terms:

Some important ITIL terms are defined below:

Service Design/Transition/Operation are part of **Progressive phases**, Service Strategy belongs to **Policies and Objectives phase**, and Continual Service Improvement belongs to **Learning and Improvement phase**.

Service Strategy & Continual Service Improvement provide **Lifecycle Governance** whereas, Service Design, Transition, and Operation provide **Lifecycle Operation.**

Each service includes various Processes.

What is a Process? Activities to implement resources/capabilities to produce desired outcome, which directly/indirectly creates value to customer/business. A process may include policies, standards, templates, guidelines, instructions, roles/responsibilities, tools, controls, inputs, outputs, and activities. Processes are **Closed-Loop** systems, where you learn from experience and use that as a feedback to improve next set of processes over time.

Three most important factors for a process are **Effectiveness**, **Efficiency**, and **Consistency** i.e.
- A process is effective when it achieves planned outcome
- Efficiency can be of two types i.e.
    Internal Efficiency: Same as productivity i.e. how many resources/costs are used to provide a service
    External Efficiency is related to the **Value** influenced by business outcomes, and may be decided by perception, preference, and mindset of the customer - this may be more important since that's what is the desired outcome

- If sometimes it takes 30 minutes to perform a service, sometimes 2 hours under similar situation, then it will become difficult to anticipate, so plan accordingly. Consistency is based upon least variations (like standard deviation).

Manufacturing/Marketing Mindset

In a Manufacturing mindset, the company is building a generic product for a category of potential customers, whereas in a Marketing Mindset, the product is customized based upon customer requirements.

Market Spaces

Set of outcomes needed by customers, which can be supported by one or more services.

Utility (Fitness for Purpose)

Functionality provided that either enhances performance or reduces constraints. Examples being to support all servers, to support specific applications, to provide oil change etc.

Warranty (Fitness for Use)

Includes facilities like consistency, availability, capacity, security. Main purpose is to minimize performance variation. An example - a server should work 99.9% of the time

Service Assets:

Bundles of resources and capabilities, owned and managed by the service provider

Customer Assets:

Affects the performance of customer assets. Includes – employees, business processes, applications, documents, transactions

Service Providers:

An IT service provider is responsible for the IT service provision

Service Provider Types

- **Type 1 (Internal Service Provider)** i.e. an internal service provider for a specific group like service provider for a particular location, or industry, or profile etc. within a company

- **Type 2 (Shared Service Provider)** i.e. an internal service provider providing service to more than one group (within the same company)
- **Type 3 (External Service Provider)** i.e. an external service provider not directly related to the same company to provide the IT service

External Stakeholders for the Service Provider

If you are a service provider, there are three main external stakeholders i.e.

- **Customer:** Typically, one who is responsible for service payment
- **User:** Although a customer may be responsible for service payment, a user is accessing the system and using the service on a regular basis
- **Supplier:** A Third party providing some services for the service provider like PC manufacturer who will maintain the PCs

Service Package:

Detailed description of an IT service to be delivered to customers that includes two main service types i.e.

Core Services: Basic outcomes desired by customer, they are willing to pay

Supporting Services: Either enable or enhance the value of a service

- **Enabling Services** are basic factors/framework that qualify the provider for an opportunity to serve
- **Enhancing services** are excitement factors for differentiation

MoSCoW: Must Have, Should have, Could Have, and Wouldn't Have.

Now we will provide some details about main services and functions

Chapter 3.4.3. Service Strategy:

A guide to strategize and decide i.e. what services need to be provided, updated, or removed based upon various business assessments, and customer needs

4 P's of Strategy:

- **Perspective**: Vision and direction, like: 'We will be the best service provider for the cloud computing (SaaS)'
- **Position**: Well-defined stance. Should we compete on the basis of providing value or low-cost, utility or warranty, specialty or broad-based
- **Plan**: Means of transitioning from 'as-is' to 'to-be'
- **Pattern**: Series of consistent decisions and actions over time

Major Processes:

Strategy Management for IT Services

Provides Strategy Assessment & Development of service strategy

Demand Management

Understand demand based upon
- Operational requirements
- Future projections
- Historic patterns
- Forecasts

Understand customer's Patterns of Business Activity (PBA)
- Attributes: Frequency, Volume, Location, Duration
- Requirements: Performance, Security, Availability, Privacy, Latency, Tolerance for delay
- Service Asset Requirements: Resources used, Pattern of Utilization

Service Portfolio Management

Complete set of services that are managed by a service provider. Includes cost and other internal details for all service states – shown below.

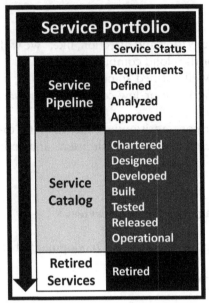

Fig 3.4.1 Service Portfolio

Financial Management
- Provides operational visibility, insight, and better decision making
- Quantify IT services, the value of the assets, and qualify operational forecasting
- Ensure proper funding

Cost Categories:
- **Capital/Operational:**
  Capital: Initial expense (Infrastructure/Real estate…)
  Operational: Ongoing expenses
- **Direct/Indirect:**
  Direct: Directly related to service (Lawn Mower for Lawn mowing)
  Indirect: Common across various services (Travel expenses, Real estate)
- **Fixed/Variable:**
  Fixed: Not directly proportional to usage (Server cost)
  Variable: Depend upon the degree of service (Hourly cost)

Business Relationship Management
- Maintain Customer Relationships
- Identify Service Requirements
- Sign up Customers to Standard Services
- Customer Satisfaction Survey
- Handle Customer Complaints
- Monitor Customer Complaints

Chapter 3.4.4. Service Design:

Once Service Strategy decides which service to be provided, Service Design will provide that service under development environment

Design is the art of applying constraints until only one solution remains. Keep applying more and more conditions/rules till one best solution is achieved – as shown in the diagram below.

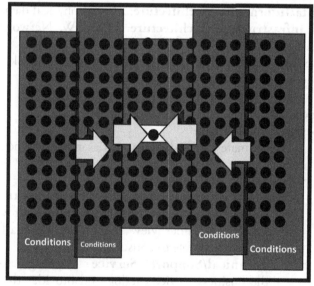

Fig 3.4.2 Service Design

Major Design Aspects (STAMP) – Design of
- Service solutions
- Tools
- Architecture
- Measurement systems
- Processes

Asset Types
- IT Infrastructure
- Applications
- Information
- People

4 Ps of design
- People
- Process
- Products
- Partners

Architecture: Structure of an IT service, relationship of components, their environment, standards and guidelines.
- **Service Architecture:** Translates activities into sets of services
- **Application Architecture:** Development & deployment of applications
- **Data/Information Architecture:** Logical/physical data assets.
- **IT infrastructure Architecture:** HW, SW, Networking and Relationships
- **Environment Architecture:** Environment controls like heating/air conditioning etc.

Major Processes
Design Coordination
Coordinate service design activities, processes and resources

Service Catalog Management
Service Catalog portion of Service Portfolio with
- **Business/Customer Service Catalog:** Provides the service consumer view that contains details of the services available to consumers
- **Technical/Support Service Catalog:** underpins the business service catalog and provides the IT view accordingly

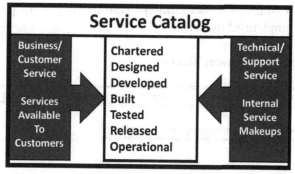

Fig 3.4.3 Service Catalog

Service Level Management

Maintain alignment of business/IT

Customer focused

SLA (Service Level Agreements) with – service description, hours, response, availability, security, continuity, service provider responsibility, exceptions

Capacity Management

Provides current & future capacity & performance aspects of the business requirements with cost effectiveness

Availability Management

Provides level of service availability as per agreement. Refer to the diagram below for some of the abbreviations

- **Availability**: Percent of agreed upon service hours i.e. (AST-DT) * 100/AST (AST-Agreed Service Time, DT-Down Time)
- **Reliability**: Ability to keep services operational i.e.
- (MTBSI in hours) = (AST in hours – DT in hours)/number of breaks.
- **Resilience**: Capability of a set of CIs to stay operational when one/more component CIs fail (CI-Configuration Item) Resilience is often provided using redundancy, fault tolerance, and duplexing
- **Maintainability** (MTRS): Ability to restore service to normalcy
- **Serviceability**: Availability of underpinning services
- **Security**: Confidentiality, Integrity, and Access
- **High Availability**: Transparency of problem to customer
- **Continuous Operation**: Transparency of planned downtime

- **Continuous Availability**: Transparency of all planned and unplanned downtimes

Availability Management Times

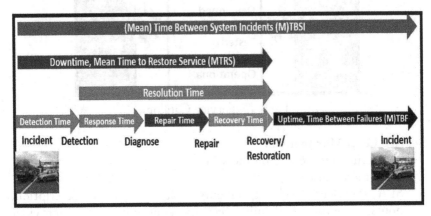

Fig 3.4.4 Availability Management Times

The Availability is MTBF/(MTBF + MTTR) for scheduled up time.

(MTBF stands for Mean Time Between Failures, MTTR stands for Mean Time To Repair)

IT Service Continuity Management
Ensure that required IT services can be recovered within required/ agreed upon time frame

Information Security Management
Provide Security per SLAs

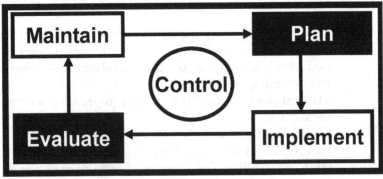

Fig 3.4.5 Information Security Management

Security Controls for threats/incidents
- Preventive - prevent
- Reductive – advance measures to reduce damage
- Detective – discover ASAP
- Repressive – Counteract any continuation/repetition
- Corrective – Corrective measures to repair ASAP

Supplier Management

Maintain Supplier/Contract Management Information System (SCMIS) and optimize their utilization for services

Chapter 3.4.5. Service Transition:

Once Service Design will complete a service under development environment, Service Transition transfers that service from development environment to production environment

Major Processes:
Service Transition Planning and Support
- Plan capacity/resources for the transition
- Support the transition team
- Ensure integrity during transition
- Communicate issues/risks/deviations

Change Management
- Respond to customer changes
- Record all changes

Change: Addition, modification, removal of anything that can impact an IT service

Type of Change Requests
- RFC (Request for Change)
- Service Desk Call
- Project Initiation Document

Three types of RFC

- **Normal Change:** Typical change requests that may need to be authorized by Change Advisory Board (CAB) and go through its process, like add an infrastructure, new application etc.

Typical processes to follow:
- Create/Record RFC
- Change Logging
- Review RFC (checking)
- Access/Evaluate the Change
- Authorize Change
- Coordinate Change, Build, and Test
- Authorize Change Deployment
- Coordinate Change Deployment
- Review and Close Change Record

- **Standard Change:** Pre-authorized (with least impact), like change password, authorize a user. These may not need authorization and may go through simple processes.
- **Emergency Change:** Risk of delaying may be more than going through long processes including authorization and there needs no 'Change Advisory Board' authorization
  Seven R's of change management:
  - Who **Raised** the change
  - **Reason** for change
  - **Return** required from change
  - **Risks** involved with change
  - **Resources** required
  - Who is **Responsible**
  - **Relationship** with other changes

Service Asset and Configuration Management

- Support efficiency/effectiveness by providing accurate information about assets and configuration items (CIs)
- Provide logical model of the services, assets, and various physical/logical components, and their relationships
- Define/control service components/infrastructure
- Enable compliance to corporate governance

Definitive Software Library (DSL): Stores/tracks authorized software CIs
Definitive Hardware Store (DHS): Stores/tracks hardware spares

Configuration Item (CI)

Any component that needs to be managed in order to deliver an IT service.

- Information about CI is recorded within the CMS (Configuration Management System) and each CI is under the control of change management
- CIs vary in complexity
- Various types of CIs include:
  - **Service CI**: Service Capability Asset, resource asset, service package, service model
  - **Organization CI**: Organizational business strategy
  - **Internal CI**: Hardware, Software
  - **External CI**: External customer requests/agreement, external service

Service Knowledge Management System (SKMS)

Set of tools/databases that are used to manage knowledge and information. SKMS stores, manages, updates, and presents all information that an IT service provider needs to manage full IT service lifecycle

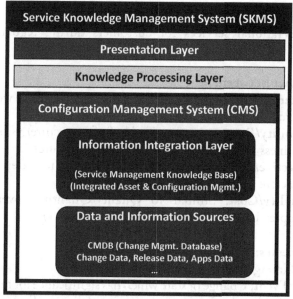

Fig 3.4.6 Service Knowledge Management System (SKMS)

Release and Deployment Management

Deploy releases into production

Deployment Options:
- Big-bang vs. Phased Approach
- Push vs. Pull Approach

- Automation vs. Manual Approach

Service Validation and Testing
Ensure appropriate levels of testing are performed during release, build, and deployment activities

Knowledge Management

- How data/information will be used
- Decision support knowledge
- Legal requirements
- Data relevance
- Cost of data capture
- Intellectual property rights

Chapter 3.4.6. Service Operation:

Once Service transitions to production environment, Service Operation provides operational services for customers during regular ongoing operations.

Balancing Act between:
- **External/Internal focus**: Serve the customer vs. worry about internal IT management
- **Stability/Responsiveness**: Stable (infrastructure) vs. Responsive (business requirements to change infrastructure)
- **Reactive/Pro-active**: Reactive (responds to external needs), proactive (new improvement opportunities)
- **Quality/Cost**: Similar to Quality/Quantity covered under Chapter 1.2.12 (Balance Quality vs. Quantity)

Major Processes:
Event Management
Event: Change of state which has significance for management of IT infrastructure or service delivery. Typically created automatically by an IT service, CI, or monitoring tool

Alert: Warning that a threshold has reached, something has changed, or a failure has occurred

Type of events:

- **Informational**: Events that signify regular operation: work completed, user logged on, email reached ...
- **Warning**: Events that signify unusual but not exceptional operation. Like - only 15% of disk storage left; Within 5% of deadline; Transaction took 10% more time than normal.
- **Exception**: Events that signify an exception: PC scan unauthorized software; No more disk space left

Incident Management

Incident: An unplanned interruption to an IT service, or reduction in the quality of an IT service. Failure of a CI that has not yet impacted on service is also an incident.

Workaround: A means of reducing or eliminating the impact of an incident or problem for which a full resolution is not yet available.

Incident Model: A way of predefining the steps that should be taken to handle a process for dealing with a particular type of incident.

Incident Lifecycle: Full lifecycle of an incident to check availability.

Major Incident: High Impact and greater urgency. It's important to track the impact and urgency to prioritize an incident.

Access Management

Manage confidentiality, availability, and integrity of data and intellectual property as defined in Information Security Management policies

- **Access**: Level/extent of a service, a user is entitled to use
- **Identity**: Unique name used to identify a user
- **Rights** (Privileges): Permissions granted i.e. Read, Write, Execute, Change, Delete

Request Fulfillment

Implement and fulfill the requested change to all required CIs

Problem Management

Minimize adverse effect of incidents/problems caused by errors in infrastructure to business, and proactively prevent the occurrence of incidents, problems, and errors.

Problem: Unknown underlying cause of one or more incidents. It becomes a '**Known Error**' when the root cause is known and a '**Temporary Workaround**' or '**Permanent Alternative**' has been found.

Known Error: A problem that has a documented root cause and a workaround.

Resolution: An action taken to repair the root cause of an incident or problem, or to implement a workaround.

Incident management is to restore the service to business as quickly as possible, whereas problem management is to establish, resolve, and prevent causes of the incidents.

If one gets high fever, incident management may be to provide generic medicine to reduce the temperate (like Tylenol), whereas problem management could be to analyze and find the reason for high fever and provide the treatment accordingly.

Chapter 3.4.7. Continual Service Improvement:

Ways to improve service, process as well as cost-effectiveness; and measurement of current performance to align/realign IT services to change business needs:

- One cannot manage what One cannot control
- One cannot control what One cannot measure
- One cannot measure what One cannot define

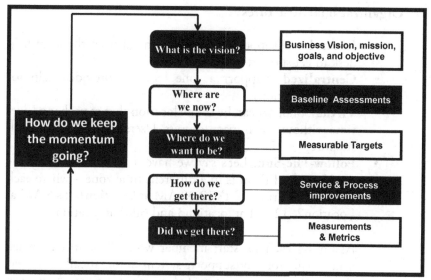

Fig 3.4.7 Continual Service Improvement

Major Processes:
    Seven-Step Improvement Process
        1. Identify the strategy for improvement: overall vision, business need, strategic/tactic/operational goals.
        2. Define what you will measure: (Where we are now and where we want to be. Create gap analysis and 'How do we get there')?
        3. Gathering the data: Did we get there?
        4. Processing the data: in alignment with CSFs (Critical Success Factors) and KPIs (Key Performance Indicators).
        5. Analyze the data/information: Who, what, when, where, and how?
        6. Presenting/using the information: Did we get there?
        7. Implementing corrective action: Wisdom applied to knowledge.

Chapter 3.4.8. Functions

A function is self-contained with resources/capabilities.

Service Desk Function

    Point of contact between a user and IT to initiate any service issue, that may drill down from Tier1 to Tier2 and so on as needed, where Tier2 provides more detailed technical help than Tier1 and so on.

Organizational Structures

- **Local**: Local support where one can call/visit the local help desk to get support
- **Centralized**: Support at one location provides help for multiple locations
- **Virtual**: Support can be at any location that may change over time without any impact to users. Users can have online/call support
- **Follow-The-Sun**: Let's say we have 4 locations around the world, each of them is in a different time zone – where each is 6 hours apart i.e. if it's 12.00 AM at Location1, it's 6 AM at Location2, 12 PM at location3 and 6PM at location4.

Assuming each IT staff member works 8 hours/day, when a user calls for any support, system automatically transfers that to the proper location (where it's day time). Moreover, it provides 2 hours per location to share any pending issues.

In other words, if each location works for 8 hours from 9 AM to 5 PM (local time), they support from 10 AM to 4 PM, and from 9 AM to 10 AM and 4 PM to 5 PM share the pending issues with previous/next location or keep records.

This way, location/timing is completely transparent to the user and any changes done for help support are fully independent.

Operations Management

- Activities to perform day-to-day IT operations
- Monitoring (Open/Close loop), Reporting, and controlling.

Includes:

- Console management
- Job scheduling
- Backup/Restore
- Print/Output
- Performance of Maintenance
- Facilities Management
- Building Management
- Equipment Hosting
- Power Management
- Environment Conditioning & Alert Systems Safety

- Physical Access Control
- Shipping/Receiving
- Contract Management

Technical Management
- Provides technical knowledge & resources

Includes:
- Maintain stable technical infrastructure
- Well designed and highly resilient technical topology
- Use adequate technical skills to maintain the technical infrastructure
- Swift use of technical skills to diagnose/resolve technical infrastructure

Application Management
- Custodian of technical knowledge related to managing applications
- Provide resources to manage applications

Includes:
- Well designed and highly resilient applications
- Use adequate technical skills to maintain the applications
- Swift use of technical skills to diagnose/resolve applications

Sub-Section 3.5

Quality/Waste Management

This sub-section covers Quality Management and Waste Management at a very high level as defined by **Six Sigma**. Main purpose of Six Sigma is to improve the output quality of a process by identifying and removing the causes of defects and maintaining consistency of the output value. Sig Sigma definition is related to Standard Deviation and restricts defects within 3.4 per million.

The data-driven quality strategy for improving process to retain the quality as expected is controlled by DMAIC (also referred as RDMAIC) or DMADV.

DMAIC (Define, Measure, Analyze, Improve, Control)

It's a cyclical process and the purpose of each process step is to ensure the best possible results.

Define: Define scope and what to expect

First you define the Customer, their Critical issues, and the Core Business Process involved i.e.

- Who are the customers, their requirements and expectations?
- What are project boundaries
- What processes need to be improved by mapping the process flow

Measure: Measure the results

Once defined, measure the performance of Core Business Processes involved

- Develop a data collection plan for the process
- Collect data from many sources to determine type of defects and metrics
- Compare to customer survey results and determine shortfalls

Analyze: Analyze the results

Once measured, collect the data and analyze with process maps to determine root causes of defects and opportunities for improvement

- Identify gaps between current performance and goal performance
- Prioritize opportunities to improve
- Identify sources of variation

Improve: Improve processes based upon results and expectations

Once analyzed, improve the target process by designing creative solutions to fix and prevent problems

- Create innovative solutions using technology and discipline
- Develop and deploy implementation plan

Control: Instead of being re-active to improve results, be pro-active to control results

Use the process steps to control future improvements by controlling the improvements to keep the process on new course

- Prevent reverting back to the "old way"
- Require the development, documentation and implementation of an ongoing monitoring plan
- Adjust the staffing, training, incentives, and other structure to pre-plan the improvements

R for RDMAIC refers to an additional pre-step to **R**ecognize at the beginning to identify the right problem to work on

The DMADV project methodology is used to **D**esign **F**or **S**ix **S**igma (DFSS) i.e.

- **D**efine design goals that are consistent with customer demands and the enterprise strategy
- **M**easure and identify characteristics, capabilities, process capability, and risks
- **A**nalyze to develop and design alternatives
- **D**esign an improved alternative, best suited per analysis in the previous step

- Verify the design, set up pilot runs, implement production process and transfer to process owner

Waste Management is also referred to as MUDA (Japanese term) that controls the wastage across 7 main areas i.e.:

1. **Transport**: Move products not needed
2. **Inventory**: Components not used
3. **Motion**: People/Equipment activities more than required
4. **Waiting**: Waiting for the next production step
5. **Overproduction**: Being produced more than needed
6. **Over Processing**: More processing due to poor tool/product
7. **Defects**: Effort involved to inspect/fix defects

Sub-Section 3.6

Summary of Business Framework

3.1 Accomplish Mission with Strategy, Tactics, Operations
The leaders decide what is the mission of the business and define the strategy, the managers drill-down that strategy into tactics that provide what to implement and when, and the teams provide means and operations to implement them. Overall purpose is to achieve success,
3.2 Sales/Pre-Sales
<ul><li>**Impress Business/Technical Leaders of Potential Customers**: Instead of providing only technical solutions, start with an overall diagram (with high level details) including all towers, drill down to a diagram for each tower and then more technical details. This may impress any client leader to drill-down to the extent desired besides minimizing gaps across towers, and add more resources over time to provide low level details as we feel high probability of bidding and save money</li><li>**Minimize Sales/Pre-Sales expense**: Reuse templates, tools, resources across sales/pre-sales</li><li>**Balance Sales/Delivery**: Besides communicating with experts, use historic factual data as a base to ensure: 1) What we promise, we are capable of delivering, 2) We don't underquote or overquote, 3) Our level of risk is correct based upon how frequently those risks have become issues in the past and quote accordingly</li><li>**Co-relate Sales/Delivery/Operations and their Historic Data**: Timesheets are captured using WBS code but Sales, Delivery, and Operations are normally independent. If we ensure the WBS code for sales is related to the delivery for the same project as well as ongoing operations, all are related and it's easy to track TCO cost/profitability</li><li>**Proof of Concept (Prototyping)**: It's important to confirm that our understanding of what the customer needs is correct. It can help impress the customer as well as our understanding of delivery and thus provide a real solution as well as higher probability of delivering proper product</li><li>**Go-to-market (GTM)**: Use customer needs as major input, ensure that we are capable of delivering it, and we will make overall TCO profitability of delivering this</li><li>**Market Dynamics**: Use historic data and current capabilities as main input to avoid underquoting or overquoting</li><li>**POV (Point of View)**: Use past history, prediction based upon past data and appropriate tools to check how realist is our promise. Moreover, use historic patterns to check the data related to our realistic approach in the past and what actually happened</li><li>**Negotiation**: Win-Lose means you win and the customer may lose, Win/Win means both win. If you are selling a product/service to a customer without any need for future relationship/selling, win-lose may be fine. However, if the customer loses, they may not be the future customer. Therefore, for potential continuity and B2B, use win-win negotiation.</li></ul>

3.3 Project Management

- **Purpose of Project Management**: Main purpose of a project manager is to deliver a project as promised what to deliver (scope), when to deliver (time), how much to spend-(cost)?
  A project may have various technical teams, internal/external teams, communications, change in customer requirements, sudden changes in availability of various resources (people, hardware, software, financial input etc.), and many more.
  Purpose of Project Management is to co-ordinate across all resources to find real-time situations, collaborate across all resources in real-time, dynamically redistribute resources as needed to maximize the possibility of delivering as promised
- **Water Fall vs. Iterative/Agile Methodologies**: Water Fall methodology delivers using multiple stages for a project (like get customer requirements, design, implement, test, deploy…). Various stages work in sequence i.e. once a stage starts, we can't go back to a previous stage.
  Iterative or Agile methodology allows various stages going in parallel, and we can go back to previous stage and improve them if we find an issue
- **Water Fall Project Management**: There are many tools related to Water Fall like PMI, Prince2, Mavenlink etc.
- **Scrum**: Scrum master manages the project. All pending tasks are captured in Product Backlog, and what do implement in the iteration is captured in Spring Backlog. Daily Scrum provides simple and short daily meeting to discuss main points
- **Rational Unified Process (RUP)**: RUP provides 4 phases (Inception, Elaboration, Construction, and Transition) across various disciplines and each phase can have multiple iterations
- **The Unified Modeling Language (UML)**: Offers a standard way to write a system's blueprint, including conceptual things such as business processes and system functions as well as concrete steps such as programming language statements, database schemas, and reusable software components. Has many different types of diagrams including Use Case Diagram

3.4 IT Service Management

- **Purpose of ITIL**: Contains standards to provide service management for Information Technology
- **Service Strategy**: What services need to be provided, updated, or removed based upon various business assessments, and customer needs
- **Service Design**: Once Service Strategy decides which service to be provided, Service Design provides that service under development environment
- **Service Transition**: Once Service Design will complete a service under development environment, Service Transition transfers that service from development environment to production environment

- **Service Operation**: Once Service transitions to production environment, Service Operation provides operational services for customers during regular ongoing operations
- **Continual Service Improvement**: Ways to improve service, process as well as cost-effectiveness; and measurement of current performance to align/realign IT services to change business needs
- **Functions**: Help Desk that includes Local, Centralized, Virtual, or Follow-The-Sun approach. Also include 3 other type of functions i.e. Operations Management, Technical Management, and Application Management

3.5. Quality/Waste Management

Main purpose of Six Sigma is to improve the output quality of a process by identifying and removing the causes of defects and maintaining consistency of the output value. Sig Sigma definition is related to Standard Deviation and restricts defects within 3.4 per million.

Main part of quality management is DMAIC i.e. Define scope and what to expect, Measure the results, Analyze the results, Improve the process, and Control the processes pro-actively.

Waste Management controls the wastage across Transport, Inventory, Motion, Waiting, Overproduction, Over Processing, and Defects.

About the Authors

Dinesh is a technologist by heart who has become a business leader over time. He is very innovative with a number of US patents (5 awarded, several pending, and many provisional), quite passionate but practical. Dinesh completed his master's degree in computers from IIT Delhi, with 20+ years' work experience, started as a developer/analyst and has been serving in various areas including technology, delivery, sales support, procurement, and people management. Dinesh truly believes that using realistic data (factual data) as a major input for any decision is extremely important, and equally important is to confirm the correctness of factual data.

Connect with Dinesh at: http://www.linkedin.com/in/dineshjindal/

Abhinav holds Masters and Ph.D. in IT from IIT Delhi, 20+ years' work experience, 2 patents, 45 published research papers, author of 'September 11: A Wake-Up Call – *scientific analysis of the problem and suggested solutions*,' (IEEE Author of the Year Award), and founder of 'Society for Universal Oneness,' (www.SFUO.org). His passion is to apply creativity in IT architecture, design, and development to solve business problems. Abhinav has rolled out several large IT digital transformations leveraging cloud and cognitive computing, integration across diverse modern and legacy applications, master data management, business process management, and is an expert at creating multi-layered architecture with end to end governance.

Connect with Abhinav at: https://www.linkedin.com/in/aaggarwal2/

Printed in the United States
By Bookmasters